PRINCESS DIANA

Biography

Dustin L VanHuss

TABLE OF CONTENTS

CHAPTER 1
In Her Own Words

Childhood

[My first memory] is really the smell of the inside of my pram. It was plastic and the smell of the hood. Vivid memory. I was born at home, not in the hospital. The biggest disruption was when Mummy decided to leg it. That is the clear recollection we have of the four of us. We all have our own perspectives on what should have happened and what actually transpired. Everyone chooses sides. Several folks did not speak to each other. My brother and I had a really ambiguous and unpleasant encounter. Charles [her brother] told me the other day that he didn't understand how deeply the divorce had affected him until he got married and started living on his own. But my other sisters grew up out of my sight. I saw them during the holidays. I don't remember it being a big deal. I idolised my older sister and used to do all of her laundry when she returned home from school. I packed her suitcase, ran her bath, and made her bed - the works. I did everything, and I thought it was great. I always looked after my brother. My sisters were really independent. We had so many different nannies. If we didn't like someone, my brother and I would poke pins in their chairs and throw their clothes out the window. We always saw them as a threat since they attempted to seize their mother's position. They were all rather young and attractive. They were selected by my father. It was quite disturbing to return from school one day and find a new nanny.

I've always felt incredibly different from everyone else, separated. I knew I was going somewhere different but didn't know where. When I was 13, I told my father, 'I know I'm going to marry someone in the public eye,' but I was thinking of being an ambassador's wife - not the top one, by any means. It was a terribly sad childhood. Parents were busy figuring things out. I'm always watching my mother cry. Daddy never told us about it. We never asked questions. There are too many changes over nannies, and everything is really unstable. Generally sad and estranged from everyone else.

At the age of 14, I recall thinking that I wasn't very good at anything and that I was hopeless. My brother was always the one taking tests at school, while I was the dropout. I couldn't see why I was perhaps a nuisance to have around, which, in later years, I've perceived as

3

being part of the [whole subject of the] boy; the child who died before me was a son, and both [parents] were insane to have a son and an heir, and then there comes a third daughter. What a bore; we'll have to try again. I've realised it now. I've been aware of it, and I now identify it, which is fine. I accept it.

I adored animals, even guinea pigs. In my bed, I'd have 20 stuffed bed animals and a midget's space, and they'd have to sleep there every night. That was my family. I was terrified of the dark and had an obsession with it until I was at least ten years old. I used to hear my brother crying in his bed at the other end of the house, crying for my mother, and he was also upset, as was my father, and it was always terrible. I could never work up the guts to get out of bed. I still remember it today.Mummy cried a lot, and every Saturday when we went up for the weekend, she would start crying, as was regular routine. On Saturday, we'd both watch her cry. 'What is the matter, Mummy?' 'Oh, I do not want you to leave tomorrow,' which was terrible to a nine-year-old. I remember the most excruciating decision I've ever had to make. I was a bridesmaid for my first cousin, and in order to attend the rehearsal, I had to be smart and wear a dress, and my mother gave me a green dress and my father gave me a white dress, and they were both so smart, and I can't remember which one I got, but I remember being completely traumatised by it because it would show favouritism.

I recall a lot of talk at Riddlesworth [Diana's preparatory school] about how a judge would come to me and ask who I preferred to live with. The judge never appeared, and then my stepfather [Peter Shand Kydd] arrived on the scene. Charles, my brother, and I travelled up to London, and I asked Mummy, "Where is he?" Where's your new husband? 'He's at the ticket barrier,' and there was this extremely attractive, lovely man, and we wanted to adore him, so we accepted him, and he was wonderful to us, spoiling us rotten. It was quite lovely to be spoiled because my particular parents were not aware of it. Basically, Charles and I couldn't wait to be independent so we could spread our wings and do what we wanted. We had become very different at school since our parents had divorced, something no one else did at the time, but by the end of our five years at prep school, everyone was. I was always different. I've always felt that I was different. I wasn't sure why. I couldn't even talk about it, but I knew it was there. The divorce allowed me to relate to everyone else who is unhappy in their family life, whether it's stepfather syndrome, motherhood, or whatever. Been there, done that. I always got along well with everybody. I went over to speak with the gardener, the local cops, or whatever it was. My father always stated, 'Treat everybody as an individual and never throw your weight around.'

Every Christmas and birthday, my father would sit us down and assign us the task of writing thank-you letters within 24 hours. And if I don't, I get into a panic. If I return from a dinner party or anyplace that requires a letter, I will sit down at midnight and write it there rather than waiting until the next morning because it would conflict with my conscience. And William now does it; it's fantastic. It's lovely when others appreciate it on the other end. We were all moved to Sandringham [the Queen's Norfolk estate] for the holidays. We used to go to see the film Chitty Chitty Bang Bang. We disliked it so badly. We disliked going over there. When we got there, the mood was always odd, and I used to kick and resist anyone who tried to force us to go, but Daddy was adamant about it since it was disrespectful. I stated that I did not want to see Chitty Chitty Bang Bang for the third consecutive year. We had a four-week holiday, so our vacations were always miserable. Two weeks, Mummy and Daddy, and the anguish of moving from one house to another, with each parent attempting to compensate in their area with material items rather than the genuine tactile items, which we both desired but never received. When I say neither of us, my other two sisters were busy at prep school and were out of the home, whereas my brother and I were pretty much stuck together.

Diana's father's illness

And he suffered a cerebral haemorrhage. He had headaches, used Disprin, and told nobody. I had a premonition that dad was going to be unwell while I was staying with some friends in Norfolk, and when they said, 'How's your father?' I responded, 'I've got this strange sense that he's going to drop down and if he dies, he'll die instantly; otherwise, he'll live.' I heard myself say this and didn't think anything more about it. The next day, the phone rang, and I told the lady it would be about Daddy. Yes, it was. He had collapsed. I was frighteningly calm, returned to London, went to the hospital, and discovered that Daddy was severely ill. They said, 'He'll die.' The brain had ruptured, and we saw another side of Raine that we hadn't expected since she effectively barred us out of the hospital and wouldn't let us see Dad. My older sister took control of it and occasionally went in to see dad. Meanwhile, he couldn't speak because he had a tracheotomy, so he couldn't ask about his other children. Who knows what he was thinking, because no one told him. Anyway, he improved and basically changed character. He was one person before, and he was definitely a different one afterwards. He has been alienated but adoring since.

On her brother

I've always thought of him as the family's intellect. I still see it. He has S-levels and other such qualifications. Because Althorp is a large town, I believe my brother was especially treasured as the youngest and only boy. Remember, I was the girl who was going to be a male. Being third in line was an excellent position to be in; I got away with murder. I was, without a question, my father's favourite. I aspired to be as good as Charles in the classroom. I was never jealous of him. I completely understand him. He is really similar to me, as opposed to my two sisters. Like me, he will always suffer. There is something about us that attracts that section. My two sisters, on the other hand, are quite content to remain separated from various circumstances.

I remember that when I went to completing school [the Institut Alpin Videmanette in Switzerland], I wrote over 120 letters my first month. I was so unhappy there that I kept writing and writing. I felt out of place there. I learned to ski, although I was not as skilled as everyone else. It was just too claustrophobic for me, even though it was in the mountains. I spent one term there. When I found out how much it would cost to send me there, I informed them that it was a waste of their money. They whipped my back. My parents said, 'You can't come to London until you're 18, and you can't get a flat till you're 18.' So I went to work with Philippa and Jeremy Whitaker, a family from Headley Bordon, Hampshire. I looked after their only daughter, Alexandra, and lived as part of their team. It was okay. I was eager to travel to London because I believed the grass was greener on the other side.

Meeting the Prince of Wales

I'd known her [the Queen] since I was a child, so it was no great deal. Andrew and Edward were not of interest to me; I never considered Andrew. I kept thinking, "Look at the life they have, how awful," so I recall his coming to Althorp to stay, my husband, and the initial impression was, "God, what a sad man." He arrived with his

6

Labrador. My sister was all over him like a horrible rash, and I thought, 'God, he must really detest that.' I stayed out of the way. I recall being a chubby, podgy, unsmart person who made a lot of noise, which he adored. After dinner, he approached me and we had a huge dance, and he said, 'Will you show me the gallery?' I was ready to show him the gallery when my sister Sarah came up and told me to push off, and I said, 'At the very least, let me tell you where the switches to the gallery are since you won't know where they are,' and I disappeared. And he was charming himself, and when I stood next to him the next day, as a 16-year-old, I was astounded that someone like that would pay you any attention. 'Why would anybody like him be interested in me?' There was intrigue. That was it for roughly two years. Sarah saw him off and on, and she got frightfully enthusiastic about the whole affair, until she noticed something else going on, namely, that when he held his 30th birthday dance, I was invited as well.

'Why is Diana coming as well?' [My] sister inquired. I answered, "Well, I'm not sure, but I'd like to come." 'Oh, all right,' that kind of thing. I really like the dance; it was fascinating. I was not scared by the surroundings [Buckingham Palace]. I thought, "What an amazing place."

In July 1980, Philip de Pass, the de Passes' son, invited me to stay at their home. 'Would you want to come and stay for a couple of nights down in Petworth? We have the Prince of Wales staying. You're a young blood; you may amuse him. So I said, 'OK.' So I sat next to him, and Charles entered. He was all over me again, which was quite strange. I thought, 'Well, this isn't very cool. I thought guys were meant to be less blatant, so this struck me as unusual. The first night we sat on a bale at this house's grill, he had just ended with Anna Wallace. I commented, 'You looked very sorrowful as you walked up the aisle at Lord Mountbatten's funeral.' I said, 'It was the most awful thing I've ever witnessed. My heart broke for you as I watched. I said to myself, "It's wrong, you're lonely - you should be with somebody to look after you." '

The next minute, he almost leaped on me, which I found unusual, and I wasn't sure how to deal with it all. Anyway, we chatted about a number of topics, and that was it. The word "frigid" did not apply. Big F when it comes to that. He responded, "You must accompany me to London tomorrow." I have to work at Buckingham Palace, and you must join me. I thought it was too much. I replied, 'No, I can't.' I wondered, 'How will I justify my presence in Buckingham Palace when I'm meant to be staying with Philip? Then he invited me to Cowes on Britannia, where he had a lot of older pals. I was really nervous, but they were all over me like a horrible rash. I felt weird about the entire situation; obviously, someone was speaking.

I came in and out and then went to reside with my sister Jane at Balmoral, where Robert [Fellowes, Jane's husband] was the Queen's assistant private secretary. I was terrified, shitting bricks. I was scared because I had never stayed at Balmoral before and wanted to do it correctly. The anticipation was worse than being present. I was fine after I entered via the front entrance. I had a regular single bed! I've always done my own packing and unpacking, and I'm constantly shocked that Prince Charles travels with 22 pieces of hand luggage. That comes before the other stuff. I've got four or five. I felt somewhat humiliated. I remained at the castle due to press attention. It was deemed a good concept. Mr and Mrs Parker Bowles were there at all of my visits. I was by far the youngest there. Charles would call me and say, 'Would you like to come for a walk, come for a barbecue?' I answered, 'Yes, please.' I thought everything was beautiful.

Courtship

Then it sort of ramped up from there, and the press jumped on it. Then it became uncomfortable in our flat, but my three ladies were fantastic, star performers with loyalty beyond comprehension. I wished Prince Charles would hurry up and get on with it. The Queen was fed up. Charles called me from Klosters and said, 'I've got something to ask you.' A female's instinct tells her what's coming. Anyway, I sat up all night with my girls, saying, 'What do I say, what do I do?' while keeping in mind that there was someone else nearby.

By that point, I'd discovered there was someone else present. I'd spent a lot of time in Bolehyde with the Parker Bowleses, and I couldn't understand why Camilla kept telling me, 'Don't push him into doing this, don't do that.' She was intimately aware of both his and our private activities. I couldn't see why we'd be staying at Broadlands. Eventually, I figured it out and discovered the proof of the pudding, and people were willing to speak with me.

Anyway, the next day I went to Windsor and arrived at 5 p.m., and he sat me down and said, 'I've missed you so much.' However, there was never anything physical about him. It was extraordinary, but I had nothing to go on because I had never had a partner. I'd always kept them away because I thought they were all problems - and I couldn't manage it emotionally; I was messed up, I reasoned. Anyway, he asked, 'Will you marry me?' I laughed. I remember thinking, 'This is a joke,' and saying, 'Yeah, OK,' and laughing. He was quite serious. He said, 'You do realise that one day you will be Queen.' And a voice inside told me, 'You won't be Queen, but you'll have a difficult role.' So I thought 'OK,' so I said 'Yes.' I said, "I love you so much. I love you so much." He stated: 'Whatever love means.' He stated it then. So I thought that was awesome! I assumed he meant it! And so he dashed upstairs to call his mother.

In my huge immaturity, I assumed that he was madly in love with me, which he was, but he constantly had a besotted look on his face, which was not true. 'Who was this girl who was so different?' he asked, but he couldn't grasp because his immaturity extended to that area as well. Going to work with the individuals felt like an obligation to me.

I returned to the flat and sat on my bed. 'Guess what?' They said, "He asked you." What have you said? 'Yes, please.' Everybody yelled and howled, and we drove across London in secrecy. I called my parents the next morning. Daddy was thrilled. 'How great.' Mummy was thrilled. I told my brother, who said, 'Who to?'

Two days later, I flew to Australia for three weeks to settle in and organise lists and other tasks with my mother. That was a huge disaster since I pined for him but he never called me. I felt it was unusual, and whenever I called him, he was out and never returned my calls. I thought, 'OK.' I was just being generous - 'He is really busy, this, that, and the other.' When I returned from Australia, someone knocked on my door - someone from his workplace with a bouquet of flowers - and I knew they hadn't come from Charles because there was no letter. It was just someone being very polite in the office.

Press harassment
Then it all started to escalate, as if the press was obsessively tracking my every step. I recognized they had a job, but most people didn't realise I was carrying binoculars the entire time. They rented the opposite flat on Old Brompton Road, which was a library with a view of my bedroom, which was unfair to the girls. I couldn't take the phone off the hook in case any of their family members feel unwell during the night. The newspapers used to call me at 2 a.m. because they were about to publish another story - 'Could I confirm or deny it?'

I failed [her driving test] once and then passed the second time. With the media, I always made sure to pass through the lights just as they turned red, so they were stuck. When I got in my car, they would follow me around. You're talking about thirty of them, not two. I had to leave Coleherne Court once to stay with Prince Charles at Broadlands. So we removed my linens from the bed and I exited the kitchen window, which is on a side street, carrying luggage. I did it that way. I was continuously nice and civil. I was never rude. I never shouted. I cried like a baby against the four walls. I just couldn't deal with it. I cried because I had no assistance from Charles or from the Palace press office. They basically said, 'You're on your own,' and I thought, 'Fine.'

[Prince Charles] was not at all supportive. Whenever he called me, he said, "Poor Camilla Parker Bowles." I spoke with her on the phone tonight, and she said there is a lot of press at Bolehyde. She's having a very difficult time. I never complained to him about the press because I felt it was not my place to do so. I asked him, 'How many press outlets are there?' He responded, 'At least four.' I thought, 'My God, there's 34 here!' but never told him. I was able to identify an inner drive to survive. Anyway, thank God the engagement was announced, and before I knew it, I was at Clarence House [the Queen Mother's London mansion]. Nobody was there to welcome me. It was like entering a hotel. Then everyone asked, 'Why are you in Clarence House?' I said that I had been told I was expected to be there. And I had just left my flat for the last time when I was confronted by a police officer. And the night before the engagement, my police officer told me, "I just want you to know that this is your last night of freedom for the rest of your life, so make the most of it." It was as if a sword had penetrated my heart. I thought, 'God,' and giggled like an immature girl. It took us almost three days to get to the Palace from Clarence House. At Clarence House, I recall being woken up in the morning by a really sweet elderly lady who brought in all of the engagement documents and placed them on my bed.

Met Camilla

I met Camilla quite early on. I was presented to the circle, but I was clearly a threat. I was a young girl, but I posed a threat. We were always talking about Camilla, though. I once overheard him on the phone in his bath on his handheld set saying, 'Whatever happens, I will always love you.' I informed him later that I had listened at the door and we had a dirty argument. When I arrived at Clarence House, there was a note on my bed from Camilla, dated two days before, that read, 'Such great news about the engagement. Let's have lunch shortly when the Prince of Wales visits Australia and New Zealand. He'll be absent for three weeks. I would love to see the ring; lots of love, Camilla. And that was 'Wow!' So I planned lunch. We had lunch, and given how immature I was, I had no idea about jealousy, melancholy, or anything like that. I had such a great existence as a kindergarten teacher; you didn't suffer from anything, and you were weary, but that was it. There was no one around to cause you distress. So we ate lunch. Very tough indeed. She said, 'You are not going to hunt, are you?' I asked, 'On what?' She said, "Horse." You're not going to hunt when you live in Highgrove, are you? I replied, 'No.' She said, 'I just wanted to know,' and I assumed that was her method of communication. I'm still too immature to understand all of the messages that come my way. Anyway, someone at his office told me that my husband had a bracelet made for her, which she still wears today. The bracelet is made of gold chain and features a blue enamel disc. It includes the letters 'G and F', which stand for 'Gladys' and 'Fred', their nicknames. I went into this man's office one day and asked, 'Oh, what's in that parcel?' He said, 'Oh, you shouldn't look at it. I answered, 'Well, I'm going to look into it. I opened it and found a bracelet, and I thought, 'I know where this is going.' I was devastated. This happened around two weeks before we got married. He answered, 'Well, he's going to give it to her tonight. So, wrath, rage. 'Why aren't you honest with me?' But, no, he [Prince Charles] cut me to death. It's as if he'd made his decision and knew it wasn't going to work. He'd discovered the virgin, the sacrifice lamb, and he was obsessed with me. However, it was hot and chilly, hot and cold. You had no idea what mood it would be, up and down. He took the bracelet at lunchtime on Monday, and we got married on Wednesday. I went to his policeman, who was back in the office, and asked, 'John, where's Prince Charles?' He responded, 'Oh, he's gone out for lunch. So I asked, 'Why are you here? Shouldn't you be with him? 'Oh, I'll collect him later.' So I went upstairs, ate lunch with my sisters, and said, 'I can't marry him, I can't do this, this is completely unbelievable.' They were great and said, 'Well, terrible luck, Duch; your face is on the tea towels, so you're too late to get out.' We made light of it. I never dealt with that aspect of things. I merely told him, 'You must always be honest with me.' On our honeymoon, for example, we opened our journals and discussed numerous topics. Camilla's photo appears twice. On our honeymoon, we have a white tie dinner for President Sadat [of Egypt]. Cufflinks appear on his wrists, two 'C's interwoven like Chanel 'C's. I realized what it was right away. Camilla gave you those, didn't she? He responded, 'Yes, so what's wrong? They're a gift from a friend. And boy, did we have a row. Jealousy, utter jealousy - and while the two 'C's are a great idea, they weren't always that intelligent. I was the only one here [while organizing the wedding] since he had left for Australia and New Zealand on tour, and you may recall the photo of me sobbing in a red coat as he left in the plane. It had nothing to do with him leaving. The worst thing had happened before he left. I was in his study, talking to him, when the phone rang. It was Camilla, shortly before he left for five weeks. I thought, "Should I be nice or just sit here?" So I figured I'd be kind and left them to it. That destroyed my heart.

The wedding
Great anticipation. I don't believe I was glad because the crowds lifted your spirits. We got married on Wednesday, and on Monday, we went to St Paul's for our final rehearsal, which was when the camera lights were turned on and we got a taste of what the day would be like. I sobbed my eyes out. Absolutely crumbled, and it was collapsing for a variety of reasons. The Camilla issue persisted throughout our engagement, and I desperately tried to be adult about it, but I lacked the necessary underpinnings and couldn't discuss it with anyone. My husband was quite fatigued, as were both of us. Big day. He gave me a very nice signet ring to Clarence House the night before, with the Prince of Wales feathers on it, as well as a very nice

card that said, 'I'm so proud of you, and when you come up, I'll be there at the altar for you tomorrow. "Just look them in the eye and knock 'em dead." I had a severe episode of bulimia the night before. I ate everything I could find, which pleased my sister [Jane], who was staying at Clarence House with me and had no idea what was going on. It was really quiet. I was as sick as a parrot that night. It was a clear sign of what was happening. I was really peaceful the next morning when we woke up at Clarence House. Must have been awake at 5 a.m. Interesting - they put me in a bedroom overlooking the Mall, so I didn't get any sleep. I was deathly calm. I felt like a lamb to be slaughtered. I knew it but couldn't do anything about it. My final night of freedom with Jane at Clarence House. Father was so excited that he waved himself stupid. We passed St Martin-in-the-Fields, and he assumed we were at St Paul's. He was eager to get out. That was fantastic.

As I came up the aisle, I searched for her [Camilla]. I knew she was there, of course. I searched for her. Anyway, I climbed to the summit. I thought the whole thing was hilarious, getting married, since it seemed so grown up, and here was Diana, a kindergarten teacher. The entire thing was ridiculous! I sobbed a lot on Monday after we finished the practice because the tension had suddenly hit me. But by Wednesday, I was OK, and all I had to do was walk my father up the aisle, which is what I focused on, and I remember being quite nervous about curtsying to the Queen. I recall being so in love with my hubby that I couldn't take my gaze away from him. I honestly thought I was the luckiest girl in the world. He was going to look after me. Was I mistaken in that assumption? So, as I walked down the aisle, I recognized Camilla, pale grey with a veiled pillbox hat, and her son Tom standing on a chair. You still remember vividly. So, there you have it; let us hope this is the last of it. When I got out of St Paul's, it was a wonderful feeling to see everyone cheering and delighted because they thought we were happy, but there was a large question mark in my head. I understood I had taken on a huge responsibility but had no idea what I was getting myself into - no notion. Back at Buckingham Palace, I took all the shots, nothing tactile. I was just roaming around trying to figure out where I was supposed to be, carrying my long train alongside my bridesmaids and pages. Got out on the balcony, and what we saw humbled us, all these hundreds and thousands of happy people. It was simply great. I sat next to him at the wedding meal, which was lunch. We didn't say anything to each other because we were both so devastated. I was fatigued from the whole ordeal.

Honeymoon

I never tried to call it off in the sense of actually doing so, but the worst moment was when we arrived at Broadlands. I thought it was just grim. I had a lot of hope, but it was dashed by day two. Went to Broadlands. On the second night, he pulled out the van der Post novels he hadn't read [Prince Charles liked Laurens van der Post, the South African philosopher and adventurer]. Seven of them attended our honeymoon. He read them, and we had to discuss them over lunch every day. We had to entertain the boardroom on Britannia every night, which included all of the senior individuals, so we never had time to ourselves. I found it tough to accept. By that point, the bulimia was at its worst. It happened four times per day on the yacht. I'd eat whatever I could find and then be ill two minutes later - I was exhausted. So, of course, that triggered mood swings, in the sense that one minute one was pleased, the next one was crying.

I recall bawling my eyes out during our honeymoon. I was so fatigued for all the wrong reasons. We went straight from the yacht to Balmoral, where everyone greeted us, and suddenly it dawned on us. My dreams were terrible. I dreamt about Camilla all night. Charles summoned Laurens van der Post to help me. Laurens didn't comprehend me. Everyone noticed that I was losing weight and becoming increasingly ill. Essentially, they assumed I could adjust to being Princess of Wales overnight. In any case, William's conception in October was a blessing. Wonderful news captivated my thoughts. Camilla has me completely obsessed. I didn't trust him; I assumed he was calling her every five minutes to ask how he should treat his marriage. All of the Balmoral visitors that came to stay just gazed at me the entire time, treating me as if I were glass. As far as I was concerned, I was Diana; the only difference was that people now addressed me as 'Ma'am', 'Your Royal Highness', and they curtsied. That was the only difference, and I treated everyone else precisely the same. Charles used to want to go on lengthy walks around Balmoral during our honeymoon. His idea of fun would be to sit atop the highest hill in Balmoral. It's gorgeous up there. I absolutely understand; he would read Laurens van der Post or Jung to me, and keep in mind that I had no idea of psychic abilities or anything, but I knew there was something in me that hadn't been awakened yet, and I didn't think this would help! So we read those, and I finished my tapestry, and he was blissfully delighted, which was fine. He was awestruck by his mother, intimidated by his father, and I was always the third person in the room. It was never, 'Darling, would you like a drink?' It was always: 'Mummy, would you like a drink?' 'Granny, do you want a drink?' Diana, would you like a drink? Okay, no issue. But I had to be reminded that this was common because I had always assumed it was the wife first - dumb idea!

Terribly thin. People began noting, 'Your bones are showing.' So that was October, and we lived up there [at Balmoral] from August through October. By October, I was about to slit my wrists. I was in a difficult situation. It poured and rained and rained, and I came down early from Balmoral to seek treatment, not because I disliked Balmoral, but because I was in such horrible shape. Anyway, I came down here [London]. All of the analysts and psychiatrists you could imagine showed up to attempt to sort me out. Put me on high-dose Valium and everything else. But Diana, who was still present, determined it was only a matter of patience and adaptability. I was telling them what I needed. They were telling me about 'drugs'! That would keep them satisfied; they could sleep soundly knowing the Princess of Wales would not stab anyone.

Pregnancy

Then I found out I was pregnant, which was exciting, and we flew to Wales for three days as Princess and Prince of Wales. That was a complete culture shock. Wrong clothes, wrong everything, wrong timing, feeling extremely unwell, carrying this child, not telling the world I was pregnant, but looking grey and haggard while still sick. I desperately wanted to make him proud of me. Delivered a speech in Welsh. He seemed more nervous than I was. I never received any praise for it. I began to realise that this was quite typical. Sick as a bird, it rained the entire while in Wales. It wasn't easy; I wept a lot in the car, saying I couldn't get out or deal with the throng. Why had they come to see us? Please help me. He answered, 'You've simply got to get out and do it. I just got out. He tried his hardest and performed exceptionally well in that regard, getting me out and allowing me to do my part. But it cost me a lot because I didn't have the energy because I was unwell from my bulimia, let alone support for him or vice versa.

I couldn't sleep or eat, and the entire world seemed to be collapsing around me. A really challenging pregnancy, indeed. Sick the entire time, with bulimia and morning sickness. People tried to put me on medicines to keep me from getting sick. I refused. Sick, sick, ill, sick. And this family has never had someone who's had morning sickness before, so every time at Balmoral, Sandringham, or Windsor in my evening gown I had to go out, but I either fainted or became sick. It was awkward because I didn't know anything because I hadn't read my books, but I knew it was morning sickness because that's what you do. So I was 'an issue', and Diana was also 'a problem'. 'She's unusual; she's doing things that we never did. Why? Poor Charles is having a difficult time. Meanwhile, he decided not to make too many suggestions. It wasn't his position to advise her. I believe I did worry about William, but the morning sickness wasn't as awful with Harry. With William, it was horrifying; practically every time I stood up, I felt terrible. But it was a combination; I couldn't tell which was which or what triggered it, but I knew it was a bother to the setup and was designed to feel that way. Suddenly, in the midst of a black dress and black tie event, I would leave to get sick and return, and they'd say, 'Why didn't she go to bed?' I felt it was my responsibility to sit at the table; duty was all over the shop. I had no idea which way to turn. I hurled myself down the stairs in Sandringham. Charles accused me of crying wolf, and I told him I was desperate and bawling my eyes out, and he said, 'I'm not going to listen. You always do this to me. I'm going to ride now. So I threw myself down the staircase. The Queen emerges, shocked and shaking; she is terrified. I knew I wouldn't lose the baby, despite being battered around the tummy. Charles went riding, and when he returned, it was an absolute discharge. He just walked out the door.

Birth of William

When we had William we had to find a date in the diary that suited him and his polo. William had to be induced because I couldn't handle the press pressure any longer, it was becoming unbearable. It was as if everybody was monitoring every day for me. Anyway we went in very early. I was sick as a parrot the whole way through the labour, very bad labour. They wanted a Caesarean, no one told me this until afterwards. Anyway, the boy arrived, great excitement. Thrilled, everyone was absolutely high as a kite – we had found a date where Charles could get off his polo pony for me to give birth.

That was very nice, I felt very grateful about that! Came home and then postnatal depression hit me hard and it wasn't so much the baby that had produced it, it was the baby that triggered off all else that was going on in my mind. Boy, was I troubled. If he didn't come home when he said he was coming home I thought something dreadful had happened to him. Tears, panic, all the rest of it. He didn't see the panic because I would sit there quietly.

[At William's christening] I was treated like nobody else's business on 4th August [1982]. Nobody asked me when it was suitable for William – 11 o'clock couldn't have been worse. Endless pictures of the Queen, Queen Mother, Charles and William. I was totally excluded that day. I wasn't very well and I just blubbed my eyes out. William started crying too. Well, he just sensed that I wasn't exactly hunky-dory.

The first overseas tour

Then it was make-or-break for me. We visited [Australia and New Zealand], namely Alice Springs. This was the real crunch, the tough part of becoming the Princess of Wales. There were thousands of journalists following us. We were gone for six weeks, and the first day we went to this school in Alice Springs. It was hot, I was jet-lagged, and I felt terrible. I was too slim. Every day, the entire world focused on me. I was in front of the newspapers. I thought this was terrible; I hadn't done anything specific, like climb Everest or do something great like that. However, when I returned from this engagement, I went to my lady-in-waiting and screamed my eyes out, saying, 'Anne, I've had to go home; I can't cope with this.' She was also heartbroken, considering it was her first job. So that first week was so unpleasant for me that I learnt to write royal inverted commas in one week. I was thrown in the deep end. Now, I prefer it that way. Nobody assisted me at all. They'd critique me but never say, 'Well done.'

When we returned from our six-week journey, I was a changed person. I was more mature, but not at all prepared for the process that lay ahead of me over the next four or five years. Basically, our tour was a huge success. Everyone always remarked to us in the car, 'Oh, we're on the wrong side, we want to see her, we don't want to see him,' and that's all we could hear as we drove through these throngs, which clearly he and I weren't used to. He took it out on me. He was jealous, which I understood, but I couldn't explain why I hadn't asked for it. I kept saying you'd married someone, and whoever you'd married would have been interested in the clothes, how she handles this, that, and the other, and you'd have built the foundation for your wife to stand on to create her own foundation. He did not notice that at all. We took William on his first foreign trip to Australia and New Zealand. This was for six weeks. That was wonderful; we were a family unit. It was a difficult mental challenge for me because the crowds were simply unbelievable. My husband and I had never seen crowds like that before, and everyone kept telling us that it would all calm down once we had our first baby, but it never did. We never fought over taking Prince William on tour. Malcolm Fraser, who was Prime Minister at the time of the tour but was no longer so, received no credit. He wrote to us out of the blue. All set to depart William. I accepted it as part of my responsibility, albeit it would not be easy. He wrote to me and said, 'It appears to me that you, as a young family, would prefer to bring your child out.' Charles asked, 'What do you think about this?' I answered, 'Oh, that would be fantastic.' He said: "Then we can do six weeks instead of four, and we can cover New Zealand as well, so it would be ideal."

I said, 'Wonderful.' It was usually assumed that I had a disagreement with the Queen. We did not even ask her; we just did it. It was really beautiful. We didn't see much of him [William], but we shared the same sky, so to speak. That was a terrific feeling for me because everyone was curious about his improvement.

Relations with the royal family:
The Queen
The relationship certainly changed when we got engaged because I was a threat, wasn't I? I admire her. I long to get inside her mind and talk to her and I will. I've always said to her 'I'll never let you down but I cannot say the same for your son.' She took it quite well. She does relax with me. She indicated to me that the reason why our marriage had gone downhill was because Prince Charles was having such a difficult time with my bulimia. She saw it as the cause of the marriage problems and not a symptom. I kept myself to myself. I didn't ask for her advice. Now I can do it myself.

I get on very well with them [her parents-in-law] but I don't go out of my way to go and have tea with them.

Prince Charles
[I was] accused very early on of stopping him shooting and hunting – that was total rubbish. He suddenly went all vegetarian and wouldn't kill. His family thought he had gone mad, and he was ostracised within the family. They couldn't understand it and they were fearful of the future – all the estates have things that need to be shot on them. So if the heir wasn't going to take an interest, panic was going to set in. It was an influence well before me, but it all came back eventually in his own time. He does that – he has these crazes and then he drops them.

[Charles's clothes] He had an awful lot but he had very little. For instance, he had ghastly Aertex pyjamas that were honestly, simply hideous, so I bought him a silk pair, that sort of thing – and shoes. Yes, they were well received. He was absolutely thrilled.

[Charles as a father] He loved nursery life and couldn't wait to get back and do the bottle and everything. He was very good, he always came back and fed the baby. I [breast] fed William for three weeks and Harry for eleven weeks.

Queen Mother

[The Queen Mother's 90th birthday] Grim and stilted. They are all anti me. My grandmother [Ruth, Lady Fermoy] has done a good hatchet job on me.

Prince Philip and Prince Charles

Very tricky, very tricky. Prince Charles longs to be patted on the head by his father while father longing to be asked advice instead of Prince Charles giving advice.

Prince Andrew

Andrew was very, very noisy and loud. It occurred to me that there was something troubling him. He wasn't for me. Andrew was very happy to sit in front of the television all day watching cartoons and videos because he's not a goer. He doesn't like taking exercise – he loves his golf and it's rather touching. But he gets squashed by his family the whole time. He's dismissed as an idiot but actually there's a lot more that hasn't risen yet. He's very shrewd and astute.

Sweet Koo adored him. She was terribly good to have around. Very gentle and looked after him. Very quiet, devoted all her energies to him. Suited each other so well. Met her lots of times.

Princess Anne

We're always supposed to have had this tricky relationship. I admire her enormously. I keep out of her way but when she's there I don't rattle her cage and she's never rattled mine and the fuss about her being godmother to Harry was never even thought about. I thought to myself 'There's no point having anyone in the family as godparents as they are either aunts or uncles.' I said: 'The press will go for that,' and Charles said: 'So what?' They had this great thing about her and I not getting on. We get on incredibly well, but in our own way. I wouldn't ring her up if I had a problem, nor would I go and have lunch with her but when I see her it's very nice to see her. Her mind stimulates me, she fascinates me, she's very independent and she's gone her own way.

Other royals

I've always adored Margo [Princess Margaret], as I call her. I love her to bits and she's been wonderful to me from day one. Everyone keeps themselves to themselves. The Gloucesters – they are a very shy couple anyway. Feel sorry for her [the Duchess of Kent]. Would look after her if I had to.

Diana's mother and the royal family

Whenever I mention my mother's name within the royal family, which I barely do, they come on me like a ton of bricks. So I can never do anything in that department. They're convinced she's the baddie and that poor Johnnie [her father] had a very rough time.

Years of suffering

I think an awful lot of people tried to help me because they saw something going wrong but I never leant on anyone. None of my family knew about this at all. Jane, my sister, after five years of being married, came to check on me. I had a V-neck on and shorts. She said: 'Duch [Diana's childhood nickname], what's that marking on your chest?' I said: 'Oh, it's nothing.' She said: 'What is it?' And the night before I wanted to talk to Charles about something. He wouldn't listen to me, he said I was crying wolf. So I picked up his penknife off his dressing table and scratched myself heavily down my chest and both thighs. There was a lot of blood and he hadn't made any reaction whatsoever.

[On other suicide attempts] I was running around with a lemon knife, one with the serrated edges. I was just so desperate. I knew what was wrong with me but nobody else around me understood me. I needed rest and to be looked after inside my house and for people to understand the torment and anguish going on in my head. It was a desperate cry for help. I'm not spoiled – I just needed time to adapt to my new position. I don't know what my husband fed her [the Queen]. He definitely told her about my bulimia and she told everybody that was the reason why our marriage had cracked up because of Diana's eating and it must be so difficult for Charles. It was at the Expo [in Canada] where I passed out. I remember I had never fainted before in my life. We'd been walking around for four hours, we hadn't had any food and presumably I hadn't eaten for days beforehand. When I say that, I mean food staying down. I remember walking around feeling really ghastly. I didn't dare tell anyone I felt ghastly because I thought they'd think I was whinging.

I put my arm on my husband's shoulder and said: 'Darling, I think I'm about to disappear,' and slid down the side of him. Whereupon David Roycroft and Anne Beckwith-Smith [royal aides] who were with us at the time took me to a room. My husband told me off. He said I could have passed out quietly somewhere else, behind a door. It was all very embarrassing. My argument was I didn't know anything about fainting. Everyone was very concerned. I fainted in the American section. While Anne and David were bringing me round, Charles went on around the exhibition. He left me to it. I got back to the hotel in Vancouver and blubbed my eyes out. Basically I was overtired, exhausted and on my knees because I hadn't got any food inside me. Everyone was saying: 'She can't go out tonight, she must have some sleep.' Charles said: 'She must go out tonight otherwise there's going to be a sense of terrific drama and they are going to think there's something really awful wrong with her.' Inside me I knew there was something wrong with me but I was too immature to voice it. A doctor came and saw me. I told him I was being sick. He didn't know what to say because the issue was too big for him to handle. He just gave me a pill and shut me up.

It was all very strange, I just felt miserable. I knew the bulimia started the week after we got engaged. My husband put his hand on my waistline and said: 'Oh, a bit chubby here, aren't we?' and that triggered off something in me – and the Camilla thing, I was desperate, desperate. I remember the first time I made myself sick. I was so thrilled because I thought this was the release of tension. The first time I was measured for my wedding dress I was 29 inches around the waist. The day I got married I was 23½ inches. I had shrunk into nothing from February to July. I had shrunk to nothing. On the outside, people were saying I gave my husband a hard time, that I was acting like a spoiled child, but I knew I just needed rest and patience and time to adapt to all the roles that were required of me overnight. By then there was immense jealousy because every single day I was on the front of the newspapers. I read two newspapers, albeit I was always supposed to have read them all. I did take criticism hard because I tried so hard to show them that I wasn't going to let them down, but obviously that didn't come across strongly enough at that point. We had a few trying to cut wrists, throwing things out of windows, breaking glass. I threw myself downstairs when I was four months pregnant with William, trying to get my husband's attention, for him to listen to me. But he just said, 'You're crying wolf.'

I gave everybody a fright. I couldn't sleep, I just never slept. I went for three nights without any sleep at all. I had no fuel to sleep on. I thought my bulimia was secret but quite a few of the people in the house recognized it was going on, but nobody mentioned it. They all thought it was quite amusing that I ate so much but never put any weight on. I always kept my breakfast down. I don't know what the hell it was. I didn't take vitamin pills. I just got help from somewhere – I don't know where it came from. I swam every day, I never went out at night, I didn't burn candles at both ends. I got up very early in the morning, on my own, to be on my own and at night-time went to bed early, so it wasn't as though I was being a masochist to my system but not to my energy level. I always had terrific energy – I've always had. It went on and on. Only a year and a half ago I suddenly woke and realised that I was on the way down fast. I just cried at every opportunity which thrilled people in a way because when you're crying in this system you are weak and 'Good, we can handle it.' But when you bounce up again, 'What the hell has happened?' questions again. The public side was very different from the private side. The public side, they wanted a fairy princess to come and touch them and everything would turn into gold and all their worries would be forgotten. Little did they realise that the individual was crucifying herself inside, because she didn't think she was good enough. 'Why me, why all this publicity?' My husband started to get very jealous and anxious by then, too. Inside the system I was treated very differently, as though I was an oddball and I felt I was an oddball, and so I thought I wasn't good enough. But now I think it's good to be the oddball, thank God, thank God, thank God!

I had so many dreams as a young girl that I wanted, and hoped that and the other, that my husband would look after me. He would be a father figure and he'd support me, encourage me, say 'Well done,' or say 'No, it wasn't good enough,' but I didn't get any of that. I couldn't believe it, I got none of that, it was role reversal.

The turning-point [in Klosters, Switzerland in 1988]

We took off skiing. I had the flu and had been in bed for two days. Three days in bed. Fergie returned in the afternoon, at 2.30pm. She was four or five months pregnant with Beatrice at the time. She crashed upside down in a ditch and emerged scared, pallid, and

23

weary. I put her to bed, and both of us were in the chalet when we heard this helicopter take off. I told her there had been an avalanche, and she replied, "Something went wrong."

We heard Philip Mackie [royal aide] enter the chalet. He wasn't aware that the two girls were upstairs. We heard him say, 'There's been an accident,' and I called down, 'Philip, what's going on?' 'Oh, nothing at all; we'll inform you soon.' I said, 'Tell us immediately.' He said, 'There was an accident, and one of the party members died.' So Fergie and I sat there, on top of the stairs, and had no idea who it was. Half an hour later, it was revealed that it was a male, and three-quarters of an hour later, Charles called Fergie to inform her that it was not him, but Hugh [Major Hugh Lindsay, a former equerry to the Queen]. That completely flipped me inside out. So everyone began shaking. They weren't sure what to do next. I told Fergie, 'Right, we must hurry upstairs and pack Hugh's suitcase right now, while we don't know what's going to happen. We must take out the passport and hand it over to the police. And we walked upstairs to pack everything. I brought the bag downstairs and told Tony [Prince Charles' bodyguard], 'I've put the suitcase under your bed. It's there when you need it, but we'd like Hugh's stuff returned so we can give them to Sarah [Major Lindsay's wife], including his signet ring and watch.' I felt awfully in command of the entire situation. I told my husband, 'We're going home to bring the body home to Sarah; we owe it to Sarah.' Anyway, there were a lot of disagreements regarding that. I asked my cop to get Hugh's body out of the hospital. Anyway, we returned from Klosters. We got back at Northolt with Hugh's coffin in the bottom of the plane, and Sarah was waiting there, six months pregnant, and it was a dreadful image, just awful. We had to watch the coffin come out, and then Sarah came to stay with me at Highgrove when I was on my own, and she cried from dawn to dusk, and my sister came, and every time we mentioned the name of Hugh, there were tears, tears, but I thought it was good to mention his name because she had to cleanse herself of it, and her grief went long and hard, because he was killed in a foreign country, she wasn't out there with him, they'd only been married eight months, she was The whole incident was horrifying, and what a great person he was. He should not have been among those who went. Fergie and I were closer to Hugh than to Charles. He got along well with everyone in my husband's family and was always a star performer. I took command there. My spouse made me feel so inadequate in every aspect that every time I came up for air, he pulled me back down. When my bulimia was over two years ago, I felt so much stronger psychologically and physically that I was able to go on in the world. Even if I ate a lot of dinner, Charles would ask: "Is that going to reappear later?" What a waste! He told my sister, 'I'm worried about Di; she's not sleeping; can't you talk to her?' I suppose he's figured it out.

Long road to recovery

I believe the bulimia truly woke me up. I instantly realised what I stood to lose if I let go, and was it worth it? Carolyn Bartholomew called me one night and said, "Do you know that if you eat potassium and magnesium, you get these hideous depressions?" I replied, 'No.' 'So, surely that is what you suffer from; have you told anyone?' I replied, 'No.' 'You must inform a doctor.' I said, 'I can't.' She continued, 'You must, I'll give you one hour to call your doctor, and if you don't, I'll tell the world. She was furious with me, which is how I became engaged with the psychologist Maurice Lipsedge. He came along, a darling and really charming. He went in and asked, "How many times have you tried to do it yourself?" I thought, 'I don't believe this question,' so I heard myself respond 'Four or five times'. He asked all these questions, and I was able to be completely honest with him. After a few hours, he said, 'I'm going to come and visit you once a week for an hour, and we're just going to talk it out.' He helped me rebuild my self-esteem and offered me literature to read. I kept thinking, 'This is me, this is me; I'm not alone.'

Dr. Lipsedge stated, "In six months, you won't recognize yourself." If you can keep your food down, you will radically alter. I must say that it's been like being born again since then, with only rare bursts, particularly at Balmoral (extremely awful at Balmoral), Sandringham, and Windsor. Sick the entire time. Last year, it was once every three weeks, compared to four times a day, which was a huge 'hooray' on my behalf. My skin and teeth were unaffected. When you think about all the acid! I was amazed by my hair.

I despised myself so much that I didn't think I was good enough, not good enough for Charles, not good enough as a mother - I had doubts as long as a leg.

I've got what my mother has. You can put on the most incredible show of happiness no matter how bad you feel. My mother is a master at this. I picked it up and held the wolves at bay, but what I couldn't bear in those dark days was people saying, 'It's her fault.' I got that from everybody, even the system, and the media began to blame me - 'I was the Marilyn Monroe of the 1980s and I was adoring it.' I've never sat down and exclaimed, 'Hooray, how fantastic,' because if I do, we're in trouble in this setup. As my time permits, I am carrying out a duty as the Princess of Wales. Life is unpredictable, but I believe I will end my 12-15 years as Princess of Wales. I don't see it anymore, oddly enough.

From the beginning, I knew I would never be the next Queen. No one said it to me; I just knew. I consulted an astrologer six years ago. 'I've had to get out, I can't take it any longer,' I told her, and she answered, 'One day you'll be permitted out, but not by divorcing or anything like that.' that's always been in my head; she told me that in 1984, so I've known that for a while. There was no praise; I'd go to dinner and he'd say, 'Oh, not that dress again,' or something like that, but one of the most daring times of my entire ten years was when we went to this terrible party for Camilla's sister's 40th birthday. Nobody expected me to show up, but a voice inside me urged, 'Go for the hell of it.' So I psyched myself up terribly. I chose not to kiss her, but instead shake her hand. And I was feeling frightfully courageous and bold, and Diana was going to come away having done her part. He needled me all the way down to Ham Common, where the party was held. 'Oh, why are you coming tonight?' - Needle, needle, needle, all the way down. I did not bite, but I was on edge. Anyway, I walk into the house, extend my hand to Camilla for the first time, and think, 'Phew, I've gotten over that. We all sat down, and, given that they were all my husband's age, I felt completely out of place, but I resolved to give it my all. I was going to have an impact. After dinner, we all went upstairs, and I was talking away when I saw Camilla and Charles were not there. So this disturbed me, and I made my way downstairs. I know what I'm going to confront myself with. They tried to prevent me from going downstairs. 'Diana, don't go down there.' 'I'm just going to find my hubby; I want to see him.' I'd been upstairs for an hour and a half, so I was allowed to walk downstairs and locate him. I go downstairs, and there is a pretty happy little threesome chatting away: Camilla, Charles, and another man. So I thought, "Right, this is your moment," and joined in the conversation as if we were all best friends, until the other man said,

"I think we should go upstairs now." So we rose up and I said: 'Camilla, I'd want to have a word with you if it's possible,' and she looked really uncomfortable and put her head down, and I said to the men: 'Boys, I'm just going to have a quick chat with Camilla,' and 'I'll be up in a minute,' and they dashed upstairs like chickens with no heads, and I could feel all hell coming loose. What is she going to do? Camilla asked, 'Would you like to sit down?' So we sat down, and I was afraid, and I said, 'Camilla, I would just like you to know that I know exactly what is going on between you and Charles, and I wasn't born yesterday. Someone was sent down to relieve us, clearly saying, 'Go down there, they're fighting.' It wasn't an argument - it was deathly calm, and I told Camilla, 'I'm sorry I'm in the way; I obviously am, and it must be awful for both of you, but I know what's going on. 'Do not treat me like an idiot.' So I went upstairs, and everyone started to depart. On the drive back, my husband was all over me like a horrible rash, and I cried like I'd never cried before - it was rage, seven years of pent-up anger gushing out. I sobbed and cried and did not sleep that night. And the next morning, when I awoke, I sensed a huge shift. I'd done something, expressed what I felt, the same envy and wrath swilling around, but it wasn't as deathly as before, and I told him three days later: 'Darling, I'm sure you'll want to know what I said to Camilla. There is no secret. You can ask her. I merely stated I loved you; there's nothing wrong with that. I answered, 'That's what I told her; I have nothing to conceal; I'm your wife and the mother of your children.' That was it; it was a huge stride for me. I was keen to know what she said to him, but I had no idea! He told many people that the reason the marriage was so shaky was because I was unwell the entire time. They never questioned how it was affecting me. Diana's sister. Jane is incredibly solid. When you call with a problem, she becomes irritated and says, 'Golly, gee, Duch, how horrible, how sad, and how awful'. But my sister Sarah vows, 'Poor Duch, such a nasty thing to happen.' My father adds, 'Just know, we will always adore you.' But that summer [1988], when I made so many mistakes, I sat down in the autumn, when I was in Scotland, and I remember telling myself, 'completely, Diana, it's no good, you've got to change it completely around, this publicity, you've got to grow up and be responsible. You have to accept that you cannot do what other 26- and 27-year-olds are doing. You've been assigned to a role, therefore you must adjust and cease resisting it. I recall our talk so vividly, sitting by the lake. I always sit near the lake while I'm thinking about anything. Stephen Twigg, a therapist who sees me, once said, 'Whatever anybody else thinks of you is none of your business.' That sat with me. When I mentioned I had to go up to Balmoral, they responded, 'Well, you've got to put up with them, but they've also got to put up with you. This story about me loathing Balmoral is false; I love Scotland, but the environment drains me completely. I move up,'strong Diana'. I leave depleted of everything because they simply suck me dry, since I listen in to all of their moods, and boy, are there some undercurrents! Instead of a holiday, this is the most hectic time of year. I enjoy being out all day. I enjoy stalking. I am much happier today. I am not euphoric, but I am far more content than I have ever been. I've really gone down deep, scraped the bottom a couple of times, and come up again, and it's very nice to meet people now and talk about tai-chi, and people say, 'Tai-chi - what do you know about tai-chi?' and I say, 'An energy flow,' and all this, and they look at me and say, 'She's the girl who's supposed to like shopping and clothes all the time. She isn't supposed to know about spiritual matters. Last week [July 1991], I visited the Aids hospice with Mrs Bush, which was another stepping stone for me. I had always longed to hug folks in their hospital beds. This specific man, who was extremely unwell, began crying as I sat on his bed and he clutched my hand, and I thought, 'Diana, do it, just do it,' and I hugged him tightly, which was very poignant since he clung to me while crying. Wonderful! It made him chuckle, and that's fine. On the other side of the room, a very young man, who I can only describe as beautiful, lying in his bed, told me he was going to die around Christmas, and his lover, a man sitting in a chair much older than him, was crying his eyes out, so I extended my hand to him and said, 'It's not supposed to be easy, all this. You have a lot of rage, don't you? He answered, 'Yes. Why him, not me? I responded, 'Isn't it strange that wherever I go, it's usually people like you, sitting in a chair, who have to go through such anguish, whilst those who accept they're going to die are calm?' He remarked, 'I didn't realise that happened,' and I answered, 'Well, it does, and you're not alone. It's nice that you're genuinely near his bed. You'll learn so much by watching your pal. He was crying and clinging to my hand, and I felt so safe in there. I loathed being taken away. After I recovered from bulimia, I met a variety of people, including the elderly, spiritual folks, and acupuncturists. When I enter the Palace for a garden party or summit conference meal, I am a completely different person. I comply with what is required of me. They can't find fault with me when I'm in their company. I perform as expected. What others say behind my back is none of my concern, but when I return here and turn off my light at night, I know I did my best.

Princes William and Harry

I realise we have two boys for a reason. We were the only ones in the family who had two boys. The rest of the family had a boy and a girl, and we were the first to change, and I believe fate had a role - Harry is a 'backup' in the kindest possible manner. William will be in his position much earlier than most people believe. I want to instil in them a sense of security, rather than expecting them to be disappointed. That has made my life so much easier. I absolutely adore my children. I come into bed with them at night, embrace them, and ask 'Who loves them the most in the whole world?' They always respond 'Mummy'. I always give them love and affection; it's extremely vital. [Preparing Prince William]. I'm changing it for him in a subtle way; others aren't aware of it, but I am. I would never rattle their cage, the monarchy, because if the mother-in-law has been doing it for 40 years, who am I to come along and disrupt it so abruptly? But, by studying what I do and, to some extent, from his father, William has gained insight into what is ahead for him. He's not hiding upstairs with the governess.

The future

I believe I will take a totally distinct road from everyone else. I'm going to leave this setup and go aid the man on the street. I dislike using the phrase man on the street' because it sounds condescending. I'm not sure yet, but I'm being pushed more and more that way. I don't like glamorous occasions anymore; they make me uneasy. I'd rather work with sick folks; it's more comfortable for me. I've been optimistic about the future, but there's always room for doubt, especially when my surroundings are busy and I watch my pals enjoying themselves. I always felt odd, as if I was in the wrong shell. I knew my life would be a twisted route. What I do now, now that I've learned to be assertive, is I let a silence pass while I'm ticking away, and then I say I'd like to think about it, and I'll give you an answer later in the day, if I'm not sure, but if I am sure, and my gut instinct tells me I am, I say 'No thank you,' and nobody responds. If I could write my own script, I would hope that my husband would go away with his lady to settle things out, leaving me and the children to bear the Wales name until William ascends the throne. And I'd be right behind them the whole time, and I know I can do this work far better on my own, so I don't feel confined. I'd love to go to the opera, ballet, or see a movie. I prefer to keep it as normal as possible. Walking along the sidewalk gives me a great rush. I'm not resentful about it, but it would be lovely to go somewhere, such as Paris for a weekend, but that's not for me right now. But I know that if I follow the rules of life - the game of life - one day, I'll be able to have the things I've always desired, and they'll be much more special since I'll be older and able to enjoy them more. I don't want my friends to be hurt or think I've abandoned them, but I don't have time to sit around gossiping; I have things to do, and time is valuable. I enjoy the countryside and reside in London because I feel safe, but I hope to move overseas one day. I'm not sure why I think that, but it makes me think of either Italy or France, which is rather unsettling; not yet. Last August, a buddy told me that I am going to marry someone who is foreign or has a lot of foreign blood in them. I found it constantly interesting. I know I'll remarry or live with someone.

CHAPTER 2
'I Was Supposed To Be a Boy'

The Honourable Diana Spencer was born late on the afternoon of July 1, 1961, as the third daughter of Viscount Althorp, then 37, and Viscountess Althorp, 12 years his junior. She weighed 7lb 12oz, and while her father expressed happiness at a 'wonderful physical specimen,' there was no hiding the family's sense of anticlimax, if not outright regret, that the new arrival was not the long-awaited male heir to carry on the Spencer name. The couple had not considered any names for females because they were so excited about having a son. A week later, they decided on the name 'Diana Frances', after a Spencer ancestor and the baby's mother. While Viscount Althorp, the late Earl Spencer, may have been proud of his infant daughter - Diana was clearly the apple of his eye - his statements concerning her health could have been more polite. Diana's mother had given birth to John only 18 months before, a severely malformed and sickly baby who lived only 10 hours. It was a difficult period for the couple, and older family members put a lot of pressure on them to figure out 'what was wrong with the mother'. They wanted to know why she kept having females. Lady Althorp, aged 23, was sent to several Harley Street clinics in London for intimate examinations. Diana's mother, who was passionately proud, belligerent, and tough-minded, found the experience humiliating and unjust, especially because it is now known that the sex of the baby is determined by the father. As her son Charles, the current Earl Spencer, observed: 'It was an awful moment for my parents and possibly the basis of their divorce because I don't think they really got over it. While she was too young to understand, Diana picked up on the family's dissatisfaction, and, believing she was 'a bother', she accepted a commensurate burden of shame - and failure - for disappointing her parents and family, feelings she subsequently came to accept and identify. Three years after Diana's birth, the long-awaited son arrived. Unlike Diana, who was christened in Sandringham church and had well-to-do commoners as godparents, baby brother Charles was christened in style at Westminster Abbey, with the Queen serving as principal godparent. The newborn inherited a quickly dwindling but still enormous fortune accumulated during the fourteenth century, when the Spencers were among Europe's wealthiest sheep traders. With their money, they inherited an earldom from Charles I, built Althorp House in Northamptonshire, gained a coat of arms and motto - 'God defend the right' - and gathered a superb collection of paintings, antiques, books, and objets d'art. Spencers spent the following three centuries in the palaces of Kensington, Buckingham, and Westminster, where they held numerous State and Court roles. If a Spencer never quite reached the commanding heights, they strode confidently in the halls of power. The Spencers were Knights of the Garter, Privy Councillors, ambassadors, and a First Lord of the Admiralty, with the third Earl Spencer being considered for Prime Minister. They were related by blood to Charles II, the Dukes of Marlborough, Devonshire, and Abercorn, as well as seven American presidents, including Franklin D. Roosevelt, actor Humphrey Bogart, and, according to legend, gangster Al Capone. Their service to the Sovereign exemplified Spencer's ideals of quiet civic service and noblesse oblige. Generations of Spencer men and women have served as Lord Chamberlain, equerry, lady-in-waiting, and other posts at court. Diana's paternal grandmother, Countess Spencer, was a Lady of the Bedchamber to Queen Elizabeth, the Queen Mother, and her maternal grandmother, Ruth, Lady Fermoy, was a Woman of the Bedchamber for nearly 30 years. Diana's father served as equerry to both King George VI and the current Queen. Diana's mother's family, the Fermoys, had origins in Ireland and links in the United States, and they were responsible for the purchase of Park House, her childhood home in Norfolk. As a sign of friendship with his second son, the Duke of York (later George VI), King George V handed Diana's grandfather, Maurice, the 4th Baron Fermoy, the lease of Park House, a huge mansion originally designed to accommodate the overflow of guests and personnel from neighbouring Sandringham House. The Fermoys clearly left their stamp on the area. Maurice Fermoy was elected Conservative Member of Parliament for King's Lynn, while his Scottish wife, who gave up a promising career as a concert pianist to marry, established the King's Lynn Festival for Arts and Music, which has drawn world-renowned musicians such as Sir John Barbirolli and Yehudi Menuhin since its inception in 1951.

For the young Diana Spencer, her extensive noble lineage was more terrifying than inspiring. She never enjoyed visits to her ancestral home of Althorp. There were too many dark corners and dimly lighted passageways filled with paintings of long-dead ancestors, their eyes following her unnervingly. As her brother described, 'It was like an old man's club with a lot of clocks ticking. For an impressionable child, it was a terrifying place. We had never looked forward to going there. This sense of doom was exacerbated by the strained relationship between her gruff grandfather Jack, the 7th Earl, and his son Johnnie Althorp. For many years, they hardly grunted, let alone spoke in words. Diana's grandpa, who was abrupt and harsh but fiercely protective of Althorp, gained the nickname 'the curator earl' because he understood the history of every artwork and item of furniture in his majestic home. He was so proud of his domain that he frequently followed visitors around with a duster and once took Winston Churchill's cigar from his mouth while in the library. Beneath this irascible façade was a man of cultivation and refinement, whose objectives contrasted dramatically with his son's laissez-faire attitude toward life and charming love of classic English country gentleman outdoor hobbies. While Diana admired her granddad, she adored her grandmother, Countess Spencer. 'She was lovely, amazing, and very special. "Divine," the Princess said. The Countess was well-known in the community for her frequent visits to the sick and infirm, and she was always ready with a kind word or gesture. Diana inherited her mother's vivacious, determined personality, as well as her paternal grandmother's thoughtfulness and compassion. In contrast to the eerie splendours of Althorp, Diana's rambling ten-bedroomed home, Park House, was positively cosy, despite the staff cottages, extensive garages, outdoor swimming pool, tennis court, and cricket pitch in the grounds, as well as the six full-time staff, which included a cook, a butler, and a governesses.

The house is sizable, with trees and shrubs separating it from the road, but its dusty, sand-brick facade makes it feel dreary and lonely. Despite its intimidating aspect, the Spencer youngsters enjoyed the sprawling pile. Charles said goodbye to each room when they relocated to Althorp in 1975 when their grandpa, the 7th Earl, died. The property was eventually converted into a Cheshire Home holiday hotel for the disabled, and Diana would occasionally stop by during her visits to Sandringham. Park House was a residence full of flair and charm. On the ground floor were the stone-flagged kitchen, the dark-green laundry room, Diana's foul-tempered ginger cat called

Marmalade's realm, and the schoolroom, where their governess, Miss Gertrude Allen - known as 'Ally' - taught the girls the fundamentals of reading and writing. Next door was a room known as 'The Beatle Room', which was exclusively dedicated to psychedelic posters, photos, and other memorabilia of Sixties pop heroes. It was an unusual surrender to the postwar period. Elsewhere, the house was a snapshot of upper-class English life, with formal family portraits and regimental images, as well as plaques, photographs, and certificates commemorating a lifetime of good works. Diana's charming cream bedroom on the top floor had a pleasant view of grazing cattle, a patchwork of open fields and parkland dotted with crops of pine, silver birch, and yew. Rabbits, foxes, and other forest critters were frequently spotted on the grounds, and the frequent sea frets that delicately curled around her sash windows indicated that the Norfolk shore was only six miles away. It was a wonderful environment for growing children. They fed trout in the lake at Sandringham House, slid down the bannisters, went on long walks with Jill, their springer spaniel, played hide-and-seek in the yard, listened to the wind whistling through the trees, and sought for pigeon eggs. During the summer, they swam in the heated outdoor swimming pool, searched for frogs and newts, picnicked on the beach near their private cottage in Brancaster, and played in their very own treehouse. And, much like in Enid Blyton's Famous Five children's stories, there were always 'lashings of ginger beer' and the aroma of something delicious baking in the kitchen. Diana, like her older sisters, began riding horses at the age of three and quickly acquired a fondness for animals, particularly little ones. She had pet hamsters, rabbits, guinea pigs, her cat Marmalade, whom Charles and Jane despised, and, as her mother recalls, 'everything in a small cage'. When one of her animals died, Diana meticulously executed a burial service. While goldfish were flushed down the toilet, she would usually place her other deceased pets in a cardboard shoe box, dig a hole beneath the spreading cedar tree on the lawn, and lay them to rest. Finally, she put a homemade crucifix over their grave. Graveyards held a sombre fascination. Charles and Diana paid frequent visits to their brother John's lichen-covered grave in the Sandringham churchyard, musing about what he would have been like and whether they would have been born if he had survived. Charles believed his parents would have completed their family with Diana, whilst the Princess believed she would not have been born. It was an unresolved issue. Diana's brother's gravestone, with its simple 'In Loving Memory' epitaph, was a constant reminder that, as she later reflected, 'I was the girl who was intended to be a boy.'

Diana's childhood amusements could have sprung from the pages of a 1930s children's book, and her upbringing echoed bygone era beliefs. She had a nanny, Kent-born Judith Parnell, who walked the infant Diana around the grounds in a well-used, highly springy perambulator. Diana's earliest memory was 'the fragrance of the warm plastic' of her pram hood. The growing girl did not get to see her mother as much as she hoped, and she saw her father even less. When Diana was born, her sisters Sarah and Jane, who were six and four years older than her, were already spending mornings in the downstairs classroom, and by the time Diana was ready to join them, they had packed their bags for boarding school.

Mealtime was spent with the nanny. Simple meals were the norm of the day. Cereals for breakfast, mince with veggies for lunch, and fish on Friday. Her parents were a pleasant but distant presence, and it wasn't until Charles was seven that he sat down to eat with his father in the downstairs dining room. Their childhood was formal and restrained, which reflected Diana's parents' upbringing. As Charles recounted, "It was a wealthy upbringing from a different era, a remote way of life from your parents. I don't know anyone who raises children like that anymore. It obviously lacked a maternal figure. Yes, I am privileged, but I am not snobby. At a young age, the Spencer children were taught the importance of good manners, honesty, and appreciating people for who they were rather than their social status. Charles stated: "We never understood the whole title business." I had no idea I had a title until I attended prep school and began receiving letters addressed to "The Honourable Charles". Then I began to wonder what it was all about. We had no idea we were privileged. As children, we accepted our situation as normal. Their royal nextdoor neighbours just blended in with a social panorama of friends and acquaintances that included the children of the Queen's land agent, Charles and Alexandra Loyd, the local vicar's daughter Penelope Ashton, and William and Annabel Fox, Diana's godparents. Social ties with the royal family were intermittent, especially since they only spent a tiny portion of the year at their 20,000-acre Sandringham estate. A royal visit to Park House was such a rare occurrence that when Princess Anne announced her intention to call after church one Sunday, the Spencer household was taken aback. Diana's father did not drink, so servants quickly searched the cupboards for a bottle of something appropriate to serve their royal guest. Finally, they discovered a cheap bottle of sherry, which had been won at a church fair, sitting forgotten in the drawer.

Occasionally, Princess Margaret's son, Viscount Linley, and the Princes Andrew and Edward would come to play, but there were no frequent arrivals and departures as many have thought. In reality, the Spencer children were nervous when they received invites to the Queen's winter house. Charles had nightmares about a character named the Children Catcher after witnessing a private cinema screening of the Walt Disney film Chitty Chitty Bang Bang. Diana despised the strange atmosphere of Sandringham. On one occasion, she refused to leave. She kicked and yelled in defiance until her father reminded her that refusing to join the other children would be considered very bad manners. If someone had informed her back then that she would one day be a member of the royal family, she would have run away. If the atmosphere in Sandringham was uncomfortable, it became awful at Park House as Diana's little world crumbled around her. Sarah and Jane started boarding school in West Heath, Kent, in September 1967, just as the Althorps' 14-year marriage fell apart. That summer, they agreed on a trial separation, which Charles described as a 'thunderbolt, a dreadful shock', terrified both families, and astonished the county set. Even for a family known for spinning a drama into a crisis, this was an unprecedented incident. They reminisced how their 1954 wedding was dubbed "the society wedding of the year," with the Queen and Queen Mother in attendance. In his bachelor days, Johnnie Spencer was unquestionably the county's most desirable man. Not only was he heir to the Spencer estates, but he also distinguished himself as a captain in the Royal Scots Greys during World War II, and as equerry to the Queen, he accompanied her and Prince Philip on their historic tour of Australia just before their marriage.

The elegance displayed by a man 12 years her senior was undoubtedly part of the appeal for the Honourable Frances Roche, the younger daughter of the 4th Baron Fermoy, who was an 18-year-old debutante when they first met. Frances' trim physique, bright attitude, and love of athletics drew the attention of many young men that season, including Major Ronald Ferguson, the father of Sarah, Duchess of York. However, Johnnie Spencer won her heart, and after a brief courtship, they married at Westminster Abbey in June 1954.

They clearly took the Bishop of Norwich's comments to heart. Sarah, their first daughter, was born just nine months after he said at their wedding, "You are making an addition to the home life of your country on which, above all, our national life depends." They settled for a country life; Johnnie attended the Royal Agricultural College in Cirencester, and after a tumultuous period on the Althorp estate, they relocated to Park House. Over the next five years, they built up a 650-acre farm, a large portion of which was purchased with £20,000 from Frances' inheritance.

Tensions quickly boiled under the veneer of family peace and marital joy. The temptation to produce a male heir was constant, and Frances was coming to the understanding that a lifestyle that had appeared urbane to her in her youth was monotonous and uninspiring in retrospect. The late Earl Spencer asked, "How many of those 14 years were happy?" I thought about them all till the moment we parted. I was mistaken. We had not fallen apart; rather, we had drifted apart.

As fractures revealed in the façade of togetherness, the mood at Park House deteriorated. In public, the pair smiled, but in private, it was a different story. While the chilling silences, angry exchanges, and bitter remarks can only be imagined, the youngsters were clearly traumatised. Diana vividly recalls watching her mother and father argue violently as she peeked from her hiding place behind the drawing room door.

The appearance of a wealthy businessman, Peter Shand Kydd, who had lately returned to Britain after selling a sheep farm in Australia, served as the spark for their outrage. The Althorps first met the outgoing, university-educated entrepreneur and his artist wife, Janet Munro Kerr, at a dinner party in London. The following decision to go skiing in Switzerland together proved to be a disastrous turning point in their lives. Peter, an engaging bon viveur with an appealing bohemian tendency, appeared to have all the attributes Johnnie lacked. Lady Althorp, 11 years his junior, was so engrossed in their affair that she overlooked his periods of despair and black mood. That would happen later.

When they returned from their vacation, Peter, then 42, moved out of his London house, leaving his wife and three children. At the same time, he began meeting Frances covertly at an apartment in South Kensington, Central London.

When the Althorps agreed to a trial separation, Diana's mother relocated from Park House to a rented apartment in Cadogan Place, Belgravia. It was then that the myth of 'the bolter' emerged, claiming that Frances had abandoned her husband and four children for the love of another man. She was cast as the drama's greedy villainess, while her husband played the innocent damaged party. In reality, before she left, Lady Althorp had already made plans for Charles and Diana to live with her in London. Diana was enrolled in a girls' day school, while Charles attended a nearby kindergarten.

When Frances arrived at her new house, her children and their nanny followed weeks later, she had every reason to believe that the children would be relatively unharmed by her divorce, especially because Sarah and Jane were attending boarding school. During the school year, the younger children returned to Park House on weekends, while their father, Viscount Althorp, spent time with them in Belgravia when he visited London. These were dismal meetings. Charles' earliest recollection is of playing quietly on the floor with a train set while his mother sobbed on the edge of the bed, his father smiling faintly at him in a desperate attempt to persuade his kid that everything was fine. The family reassembled at Park House for half-term and again over the Christmas holidays. But, as Mrs. Shand Kydd later stated, "It was my last Christmas there because by now it was clear that the marriage had completely broken down."

That disastrous visit was distinguished by a lack of holiday goodwill or tidings of delight for the future. Despite his wife's strong protests, Viscount Althorp demanded that the children return permanently to Park House and attend Silfield School in King's Lynn. 'He refused to let them return to London for the New Year,' she claimed.

As the legal machinery for divorce came into action, the children became pawns in a harsh and contentious battle that pitted mother against daughter and husband against wife. Lady Althorp filed for custody of the children, with high hopes of success because the mother normally wins - unless the father is a nobleman. He has prior claims due to his rank and title.

Lady Althorp was mentioned as the 'other lady' in the Shand Kydds' divorce two months earlier, and her own mother, Ruth, Lady Fermoy, sided against her in the case, which was heard in June 1968. It was the greatest betrayal of her life, one she would never forgive. The Althorps divorced in April 1969, and a month later, on May 2, Peter Shand Kydd and Lady Althorp married in a modest register office ceremony and purchased a property on the West Sussex coast where Peter could enjoy his love of sailing.

This nasty judicial struggle left a lasting impression on children as well as adults. Despite their parents' and family's efforts to soften the blow, the children's reactions were significant. As a result, family friends and biographers have attempted to mitigate the effect. They have claimed that Sarah and Jane were barely affected by the divorce because they were away at school, that Charles, aged four, was too young to understand, and that Diana, then seven, reacted to the breakup with 'the unthinking resilience of her age' or even regarded it as 'fresh excitement' in her young life.

The truth was more terrible than many people realised. Sarah and Diana have both struggled with debilitating eating disorders, anorexia nervosa and bulimia, at some point in their lives. These disorders stem from a complicated web of mother-daughter relationships, food and worry, and, to use jargon,'malfunctioning' family life. As Diana stated, 'Parents were busy straightening themselves out. I'm always watching my mother cry. Daddy never told us about it. We never asked questions. There are too many changes over nannies, and everything is really unstable.'

Diana appeared cheerful to the casual visitor. She was always a busy, clean little girl, running about the home at night making sure all the blinds were drawn and tucking up the zoo of small furry animals that cluttered her bed - she had them her entire life. She raced around the driveway on her blue tricycle, pushed her dolls around in her pram (she always begged for a new doll as a birthday present), and helped clothe her younger brother. Her warm, maternal, loving personality, which had defined her adult life, was becoming more apparent in her daily existence. There were more regular visits to grandparents and other relatives. Countess Spencer frequently stayed at Park House, where Ruth, Lady Fermoy, taught the children card games. She demonstrated mah-jong and bridge in her magnificent home, described as 'a small bit of Belgravia in Norfolk'. Diana's perplexity, however, was unmistakable.

Nighttimes were the worst. Diana and Charles were scared of the dark as youngsters, so they insisted on leaving the landing light on or lighting candles in their bedroom. With the wind whistling in the trees outside their window and the nighttime cries of owls and other critters, Park House may be a frightening place for a child. When their father casually suggested that a killer was on the loose in the neighbourhood, the children were too afraid to sleep, listening anxiously to every noise, creak, and squeak in the darkened house. Diana painted her cuddly green hippo's eyes with fluorescent paint so that he appeared to be watching over her at night.

Every night, as she lay in bed, surrounded by her cuddly toys, she could hear her brother screaming and crying for his mother. occasionally she went to him, but occasionally her fear of the dark overpowered her maternal instincts, and she sat in her chamber, listening to Charles scream, 'I want my mummy, I want my mummy.' Then she, too, would bury her face in the pillow and cry. 'I just couldn't handle it,' she subsequently explained. 'I could never muster the courage to get out of bed. I remember that to this day.

She did not have much faith in many of the nannies who currently worked at Park House. They fluctuated with frightening frequency, ranging from sweet to sadistic. When Diana's mother learned that her nanny was spiking her eldest girls' food with laxatives as a punishment, she fired her immediately. She wondered why they kept complaining about stomach issues until she caught the woman red handed.

Another nanny smacked Diana on the head with a wooden spoon if she misbehaved, or she pounded Charles and Diana's heads together. Charles remembered kicking a hole in his bedroom door when he was banished to his room for no apparent reason. 'Children have an innate sense of fairness, and if we believe they are wrong, we will resist,' he stated. Other nannies, such as Sally Percival, were caring and empathetic, and they still receive Christmas cards from the 'children' today.

However, the work of finding a new nanny was made even more difficult because the children, perplexed and upset, believed that the nannies had arrived to replace their mother. Diana became increasingly wary of them as they became more attractive. They stuck pins in their chairs, flung their garments out the window, and locked themselves in the restroom. In fact, Charles' childhood experiences validated his decision not to hire a nanny for his own children.

Their father occasionally joined the children for tea in the nursery, but as their former nanny Mary Clarke observed, "it was very hard going." In those early days, he was not at ease with them. Johnnie immersed himself in his work for Northamptonshire County Council, the National Association of Boys' Clubs, and his cow farm. Charles recalled: 'He was quite unhappy following the divorce, essentially shell-shocked. He spent most of his time on his studies. I remember him playing cricket with me on the lawn on rare occasions. That was a wonderful treat.'

The school just recast the problem in a different mould. Charles and Diana were well aware that they were 'different'. They were the only students at Silfield School whose parents had divorced. It distinguished them from the start, as stressed by her former form captain, Delissa Needham: "She was the only girl I knew whose parents were divorced." Those things didn't happen back then.

The school seemed nice and friendly enough. It was run by headmistress Jean Lowe, who testified on Lord Althorp's behalf in the divorce case, and had a genuine family environment. Classes were small, and teachers awarded house points and gold stars for successes in reading, writing, and art. Outside, there was a tennis court, a sandpit, a lawn for netball and rounders, and a garden for weekly scavenger hunts. Diana, used to the hustle and bustle of school life, was quiet and bashful, but she had her friend Alexandra Loyd to keep her company.

Diana found the scholarly side to be somewhat puzzling, despite her clear handwriting and fluent reading ability. Miss Lowe remembers her generosity to younger children, her love of animals, and her overall helpfulness, but not her intellectual potential. She was also talented in art, but her classmates couldn't understand why she burst into tears for no apparent reason during a painting session one sunny afternoon. They recall that she dedicated all of her pictures to 'Mummy and Daddy'.

Diana was increasingly envious of her younger brother, who was recalled as a solemn' but well-behaved small boy, while she struggled through her 'tables' and Janet and John novels. 'I wanted to be as good as him in the classroom,' she said. Diana, like many siblings, got into fights, which she always won because she was bigger and stronger. Charles protested as she pinched. He quickly understood he could hurt his sister with words, relentlessly taunting her. Both parents told him not to call his sister 'Brian', a nickname drawn from a sluggish and very dull-witted snail featured in a popular children's TV show, The Magic Roundabout.

He exacted delicious revenge with the unexpected help of the local vicar's wife. Charles recalled with relish: 'I don't know if a psychologist would say it was the trauma of the divorce, but she had a tremendous issue expressing the truth because she tended to embellish things. On the school run one day, the vicar's wife pulled over and said, "Diana Spencer, if you tell one more lie like that, I am going to make you walk home." Of course, I felt triumphant because she had been rumbled.

While sibling rivalry was an unavoidable part of growing up, Frances and Johnnie's rising parental rivalry, conscious or unconscious, as they competed for their children's love, was considerably less acceptable. However, while showering their children with expensive gifts, they did not provide the passionate embraces and kisses that the youngsters desired. Diana's father, who had already established a local reputation for orchestrating spectacular fireworks displays on Guy Fawkes Night, threw a fantastic party for her seventh birthday. He rented a dromedary named Bert from the Dudley Zoo for the afternoon and watched with delight as the shocked children were taken for rides around the lawn.

Christmas was merely an exercise in luxury. Before the big day, Charles and Diana were handed a catalogue from Hamleys, a prominent toy store in London's West End, and instructed to mark which gifts they wanted Father Christmas to send. On Christmas Day, their hopes were granted, with stockings on the ends of their mattresses brimming with gifts. 'It makes you very materialistic,' Charles explained. There was one present that forced Diana to make the most difficult decision of her young life. In 1969, she attended her cousin Elizabeth Wake-Walker's wedding to Anthony Duckworth-Chad at St James' Piccadilly. Her father provided her with a nice white outfit for the rehearsal, while her mother wore an equally smart green dress. 'I can't remember which one I got in, but I remember being completely traumatised by it because it implied favouritism.'

Every weekend, Charles and Diana travelled the train with their nanny from Norfolk to Liverpool Street station in London, where their mother met them. Shortly after they arrived at her Belgravia flat, it was customary for their mother to fall into tears. 'What's the problem, Mummy?' they would ask, to which she would always respond: 'I don't want you to leave tomorrow.' The ceremony left the children feeling guilty and bewildered. Holidays, split between parents, were just as bad. Peter Shand Kydd formally entered their lives in 1969, making life more comfortable and carefree. They initially encountered him on the platform of Liverpool Street station during one of their regular Friday transfers between Norfolk and London. Handsome, cheerful, and nicely dressed, he was an instant hit, especially when their mother informed them that they had married that morning. Peter, who had made his money in the family wallpaper business, was a kind, outgoing, and easygoing stepfather. After a brief stay in Buckinghamshire, the newlyweds relocated to an unremarkable suburban property called Appleshore in Itchenor on the West Sussex coast, where Peter, a Royal Navy veteran, took the kids sailing. He let Charles wear an admiral's hat, and thus his nickname 'The Admiral' was born. Diana was dubbed 'The Duchess', a nickname her friends still use. As Charles commented, 'If you want to know why Diana was not just a pampered toff, it's because our lifestyles were so different. It wasn't all elegant residences and butlers. My mother's home was average, and we spent half of every holiday with her, so we spent a lot of time in a relatively regular atmosphere.

Three years later, in 1972, the Shand Kydds purchased a 1,000-acre farm on the Isle of Seil, south of Oban in Argyllshire, where Mrs. Shand Kydd now lives. When the youngsters arrived for summer vacation, they had a 'Swallows and Amazon' idyll, spending their days mackerel fishing, lobster potting, sailing, and, on nice days, barbecuing on the beach. Diana even owned her own Shetland pony named Soufflé. She broke her arm while riding, which made her hesitant to ride again. She was galloping on her pony, Romilly, through the grounds of Sandringham Park when the horse stumbled, and she fell off. Although she was in pain, there was no evidence that her arm had been fractured, so she went skiing in Switzerland two days later. During her vacation, her arm felt so lifeless that she visited a small Swiss hospital for an X-ray. She was diagnosed with a 'greenstick' fracture, which occurs when a child's bones bend rather than break. A doctor strapped the arm, but when she attempted to ride again, she lost her nerve and dismounted. She continued to bike as an adult, but preferred to exercise by swimming or playing tennis, which were more appropriate for life in Central London. She excelled at swimming and dancing. They served her well when her father enrolled her in her next school, Riddlesworth Hall, which is two hours away from Park House. She grew to enjoy the school, which attempted to provide a home away from home for the 120 girls. However, when she was taken there, her initial thoughts were of betrayal and contempt. Diana was nine years old and felt her father's anguish strongly. She comforted him in a motherly, sympathetic manner as he attempted to pick up the pieces of his life. His decision to move her away from her family and siblings to a strange land was viewed as rejection. She said, 'If you love me, you won't leave me here,' as her father gently described the advantages of joining a school that provided ballet, swimming, riding, and a place to keep her favourite guinea pig, Peanuts. She had won the Fur and Feather Section with him at the Sandringham Show - 'Maybe it was because he was the only entry,' she chuckled - and later the Palmer Cup for Pets' Corner at her new school. Her father also informed her that she would be with friends. Alexandra Loyd, her cousin Diana Wake-Walker, and Claire Pratt, her godmother Sarah Pratt's daughter, were also attending the all-girls boarding school at Diss in Norfolk. Nonetheless, as he left her behind with her trunk labelled 'D. Spencer' and clutching her favourite green hippo - girls were only allowed one cuddly animal in bed - and Peanuts, he felt a profound feeling of loss. 'That was an awful day,' he added, 'to lose her.'

He was an exceptional amateur cameraman and photographed Diana before she left the house. It depicts a sweet-faced girl, bashful but cheerful, dressed in her school uniform of a dark red jacket and grey pleated skirt. He also saved the email she sent demanding 'Big choc. cake, ginger cookies, Twiglets', as well as the Daily Telegraph item she gave him about academic failures who become gifted and successful later in life. Despite being modest and demure in her first term, she was hardly a goody-goody. She liked laughter and skylarks to hard work, and while she might be boisterous, she avoided being the centre of attention. Diana would never scream out answers in class or offer to recite the lessons during assembly. Far from it. In one of her first school plays, she agreed to portray a Dutch doll if she could remain silent. She was noisy with her buddies in the dorm, yet silent in class. She was a popular student, yet she always felt like she stood out. Diana no longer felt different because her parents had divorced, but because a voice inside her informed her she would be distinct from the herd. Her intuition informed her that her life would be "a winding road." I've always felt pretty isolated from everyone else. I knew I was headed somewhere different, and I was in the wrong shell. However, she enthusiastically participated in the school's activities. She represented her house, Nightingale, in swimming and netball, and she developed a lifelong love of dance. When the yearly nativity performance rolled around, she relished the excitement of putting on make-up and dressing up. 'I was one of [those individuals] who came to pay tribute to Jesus,' she recalled, amused. At home, she enjoyed wearing her sisters' outfits. Sarah owns an early photograph of her wearing a wide-brimmed black hat and a white frock. While she admired Jane, the reasonable member of the group, she idolised her older sister. When Sarah returned home from West Heath School, Diana was an eager servant, unpacking her baggage, running her bath, and cleaning her room. Her loving domesticity was recognized not just by Viscount Althorp's butler, Albert Betts, who recalls how she ironed her own pants and performed other household activities, but also by her headmistress at Riddlesworth, Elizabeth Ridsdale (Riddy to students), who awarded her the Legatt Cup for helpfulness. That success pleased her grandmother, Countess Spencer, who had maintained a close eye on Diana since the divorce. Diana was distraught when she died in the autumn of 1972 from a brain tumour. She attended her memorial service at St James' Palace's Chapel Royal, with the Queen Mother and Princess Margaret. Diana had a special place in her heart for Countess Spencer, and she honestly believed that her grandmother was watching over her in the spirit realm. Diana's otherworldly concerns gave way to more earthly considerations when she took the Common Entrance exam to join her sisters, Sarah and Jane, at West Heath boarding school, which is nestled in 32 acres of parks and woods outside Sevenoaks, Kent. The school, founded on religious principles in 1865, placed equal emphasis on 'character and confidence' as it did scholastic aptitude. Her sister Sarah, on the other hand, exhibited far too much personality for the headmistress, Ruth Rudge. Sarah was an exceptional competitor, having passed six O-levels, riding for the Hickstead school team, starring in amateur dramatic plays, and swimming for the school team. Her intense competitive streak required her to be the most flamboyant, unruly, and undisciplined girl in school. 'She had to be the greatest at everything,' according to a contemporary. While her grandmother, Ruth, Lady Fermoy, forgave her when the energetic redhead rode her horse into Park House during a visit, Miss Rudge was unable to excuse other instances of her colourful behaviour. Sarah complained that she was 'bored', so Miss Rudge advised her to pack her things and depart for a term. Jane, the captain of the school's lacrosse team, was a total contrast to Sarah. She was highly intelligent, had a hatful of O- and A-levels, and was a prefect in the sixth form when Diana came.

Undoubtedly, there was debate in the teachers' common room on which sibling the newest Spencer recruit to Poplar class would resemble, Sarah or Jane. It was a close run event. Diana admired her elder sister, but it was not until later in life that she developed a close friendship with Jane. During their youth, Jane was more likely to throw her weight and invective behind brother Charles than her younger sister. Diana's natural desire was to imitate Sarah. During her first few weeks, she was noisy and disruptive in class. In an attempt to replicate her sister Sarah's escapades, she accepted a challenge that almost resulted in her expulsion. Diana's pals, who were examining the depleting supply of sweets in their tuck boxes, requested her to meet another girl at the end of the school drive and acquire extra supplies. She accepted a dare. She was able to overcome her dread of the dark as she walked along the tree-lined road in complete darkness. When she got to the school gate, she noticed that no one was there. She waited. And she waited. When two police cars sped through the school gates, apparently called by teachers concerned about her whereabouts, she fled behind a wall. Then she observed the lights turning on all across the school but didn't think much more about it. Finally, she returned to her dormitory, afraid not only of being caught, but also of returning empty-handed. As luck would have it, a fellow student in Diana's dormitory complained of appendicitis. Diana's teacher spotted the vacant bed during her examination. The game was over. Diana had to face the music, but so did her parents. They were summoned to meet Miss Rudge, who took a dim view of the situation. Diana's parents were secretly amused that their dutiful but meek daughter had shown so much spirit. Her mother later told her, "I didn't think you had it in you."

While the incident limited her wilder antics, Diana was always up for a dare. Food was my favourite difficulty. 'It was always a good joke: let's get Diana to eat three kippers and six slices of bread for breakfast,' remembers one schoolmate. And she did. Her image as a glutton meant that, while she frequently visited the matron with intestinal issues, these incidents had little impact on her popularity. On her birthday, her pals banded together to buy her a necklace with a 'D' for Diana. Carolyn Pride, now Carolyn Bartholomew, who had the adjacent bed in Diana's dormitory and later shared her London flat, describes her as a strong character, effervescent and boisterous'.

She added: 'Jane was quite popular, pleasant, unassuming, and uncontroversial. Diana, on the other hand, was a considerably more vibrant personality. Carolyn and Diana were drawn to each other from the start since they were among the few students whose parents had split. 'It wasn't a big deal for us, and we didn't sit crying in a corner about it,' she recalls, despite the fact that other students remember Diana as a 'quiet and controlled' girl who didn't show her feelings. Diana's bedside dressing table was adorned with two images of her favourite hamsters, Little Black Muff and Little Black Puff, rather than her family.

However, she was continually concerned about her average academic performance. Her sisters proved to be a difficult act to follow, but her brother, then at Maidwell Hall in Northamptonshire, demonstrated the scholastic abilities that subsequently earned him a place at Oxford University. The gawky youngster, who stooped to hide her height, aspired to be as good as her brother in class. She felt jealous and saw herself as a failure. I wasn't really good at anything. 'I felt hopeless, like a dropout,' she admitted.

She struggled with arithmetic and science, but she was more comfortable with things that included people. She was captivated by history, particularly the Tudors and Stuarts, and while studying English, she enjoyed literature such as Pride and Prejudice and Far from the Madding Crowd. That didn't stop her from reading gooey romance novels by Barbara Cartland, who would eventually become her step-grandmother. She wrote many pieces with her distinct, well-rounded hand covering the pages. 'It simply came out of the pen, and on and on,' she explained. Diana froze as she heard the quiet of the examination hall. Her five O-levels in English literature and language, history, geography, and art all yielded 'D' ratings, indicating failure.

The success she lacked in the classroom eventually arrived, but from an unexpected source. West Heath fostered the girls' 'good citizenship' through visits to the elderly, the sick, and the mentally impaired. Every week, Diana and another girl saw an elderly lady in Sevenoaks. They chatted with her over tea and biscuits, cleaned her house, and went shopping occasionally. At the same time, the local Voluntary Service Unit scheduled visits to Darenth Park, a big mental health facility in Dartford. On Tuesday evening, dozens of teenage volunteers were bussed in to participate in a dance with mentally and physically disabled patients.

Other children assisted with hyperactive teenagers who were so distressed that simply encouraging a patient to smile was a huge success story. "That's where she learned to go down on her hands and knees to meet people because the majority of the interaction was crawling with the patients," says Muriel Stevens, who helped organise the visits. Many new school volunteers were nervous about visiting the hospital, fueled by a fear of the unknown. Diana, on the other hand, discovered that she was born to do this job. She had an instinctive relationship with many patients, and her efforts gave her a strong sense of accomplishment. It greatly improved her self-esteem.

At the same time, she was a capable all-round athlete. She won the swimming and diving cups four years in a row. Her 'Spencer Special', in which she dove into the water with barely a ripple, usually drew a crowd. She was the netball captain and played good tennis. But she lived in the shadow of her sporty sisters and her mother, who was 'captain of everything' at school and would have played Junior Wimbledon if not for an appendicitis attack.

Diana began learning piano, but any progress she made was always overshadowed by the accomplishments of her grandmother, Lady Fermoy, who had performed in front of the Queen Mother at the Royal Albert Hall, and her sister Sarah, who studied piano at a conservatoire in Vienna after her abrupt departure from West Heath.

In contrast, her community service was something she accomplished on her own, without looking over her shoulder at the rest of her family. It was a satisfying beginning. Dance provided her another chance to shine. She enjoyed her ballet and tap classes and aspired to be a ballet dancer, but at 5ft 102 inches, she was too tall. Swan Lake was her favourite ballet, which she saw at least four times while on school trips to the Coliseum or Sadler's Wells venues in London. As she danced, she could lose herself in the motion. She frequently got out of bed at night and sneaked into the new school hall to practise. Diana practised ballet for hours on end, accompanied by music from a record player. 'It always relieves a huge strain in my head,' she explained. This extra work paid off when she won the school's dancing competition at the end of the spring semester in 1976. It's no surprise that, in preparation for her wedding, she brought her former teacher Wendy Mitchell and pianist Lily Snipp to Buckingham Palace for dancing lessons. Diana spent an hour away from the demands and strains of her new job. When the family relocated to Althorp in 1975, she had the ideal stage. On summer days, she practised her arabesques on the house's sandstone balustrades, and after the visitors left, she danced in the black-and-white marble entry hall, formally known as Wootton Hall, beneath paintings of her renowned ancestors. They weren't her only audience. While she refused to dance in public, her brother and staff took turns looking through the keyhole and watching her work out in her black leotard. 'We were all quite impressed,' he explained. The family relocated to Althorp following the death of her grandpa, the 7th Earl Spencer, on June 9, 1975. Despite being 83 years old, he was very active, and his death from pneumonia after a brief hospitalisation was unexpected. It entailed significant upheaval. The girls all became Ladies, Charles, at 11, became Viscount Althorp, and their father became the 8th Earl and inherited Althorp. With 13,000 acres of rolling Northamptonshire farmland, over 100 tied cottages, a valuable collection of paintings, including several by Sir Joshua Reynolds, rare books, and 17th-century porcelain, furniture, and silver, including the Marlborough Collection, Althorp was more than just a stately home; it was a way of life. The new Earl also inherited a £2.25 million death duty bill, as well as £80,000 in annual operational fees. This did not stop him from paying for the erection of a swimming pool to entertain his children while they walked around their new property during the holidays. Diana spent her days swimming, roaming around the grounds, driving Charles' blue beach buggy, and, of course, dancing. The staff adored her; they found her warm and unpretentious, with a penchant for chocolates, sweets, and Barbara Cartland's sugary romance novels.

She excitedly awaited Sarah's arrival from London, accompanied by a mob of her sophisticated friends. Sarah, who was witty and bright, was regarded as the queen of the season by her contemporaries, especially after her father prepared a lavish coming-of-age party at Castle Rising, a Norman castle in Norfolk. Guests arrived in horse-drawn carriages, and the approach to the castle was lit with flaming torches. The magnificent celebration is still being spoken about today. Her escorts matched her status. Everyone anticipated her relationship with Gerald Grosvenor, Duke of Westminster and Britain's richest nobleman, to culminate in marriage. She, like everyone else, was astonished when he looked elsewhere.

Diana was pleased to bask in her sister's success. Lucinda Craig Harvey, who rented a property in London with Sarah and later hired Diana as a cleaner for £1 per hour, met her potential charlady at a cricket tournament in Althorp. First impressions were unflattering. Diana struck her as 'a rather hefty girl who wore terrible Laura Ashley pregnancy gowns'. She stated, "She was quite bashful, blushed often, and was very much the younger sister. She was horribly unsophisticated and absolutely not attractive. Diana enthusiastically participated in the parties, barbecues, and frequent cricket matches. These sporting battles between the house and the village concluded with the appearance of a character who could have been created by Central Casting. A strange entry in the visitors' book read: 'Rain stopped play.' Raine Spencer, who eventually became Countess de Chambrun, is more of a phenomenon than a person. With her bouffant hairdo, exquisite feathers, overflowing charisma, and dazzling smile, she resembled a countess. She was the daughter of the outspoken romance novelist Barbara Cartland, and she already had a half-page entry in Who's Who before meeting Johnnie Spencer. Lady Lewisham, and later, in 1962, the Countess of Dartmouth, was a divisive figure in London politics, when she served as a politician on the London County Council. Her outspoken comments quickly gained a wider audience, and she became a known face in gossip columns.During the 1960s, she gained notoriety as a caricature of the 'pearls and twinset' Tory councillor, with opinions as rigid as her haircut. "I always know when I visit Conservative houses because they wash their milk bottles before they put them out," said one howler, which contributed to her being booed off the stage as she addressed students at the London School of Economics. Her loud ideas, however, concealed an iron drive, intimidating charm, and a cutting turn of phrase. She and Earl Spencer collaborated on a book for the Greater London Council called What is Our Heritage? and quickly discovered they had a lot in common. Raine, then 46, had been married to the Earl of Dartmouth for 28 years. They have four children named William, Rupert, Charlotte, and Henry. Johnnie Spencer and the Earl of Dartmouth had been close friends while at Eton. Raine used her overwhelming charm on both father and son, resulting in a reconciliation between Earl Spencer and her lover during the Earl's last years. The old Earl cherished her, especially since she got him a walking stick for every birthday and Christmas, adding to his collection. The children were less impressed. She first appeared in the early 1970s, looking like a galleon full of sail. Indeed, her presence at Sarah's 18th birthday party at Castle Rising elicited much murmuring among the Norfolk nobility. Sticky's meal at the Duke's Head hotel in King's Lynn provided Charles and Diana with their first serious opportunity to examine the new woman in their father's life. Supposedly, the supper was prepared to commemorate a tax strategy that would safeguard the family riches. In truth, it was an opportunity for Charles and Diana to get to know their potential stepmother. 'We didn't like her one bit,' Charles admitted. They informed their father that if he married her, they would wash their hands of them. In 1976, Charles, then 12, expressed his anger by sending Raine a 'vile' letter, while Diana urged a schoolfriend to mail her potential stepmother a poison pen note. The discovery of a letter from Raine to their father describing her ambitions for Althorp, right before Diana's grandfather died, inspired their behaviour. Her own feelings on the current Earl did not match how Diana and Charles watched her act in public with their grandfather. Raine and Johnnie married secretly in the Caxton Hall register office on 14 July 1977, shortly after being mentioned in divorce proceedings by the Earl of Dartmouth. The children were not informed of the wedding in advance, and Charles learned about his new stepmother from the headmaster of his prep school.

A flurry of change swept through Althorp as the new mistress attempted to turn the family property into a profitable venture in order to repay the enormous debts incurred by the new Earl. To open the home to paying tourists, the stable building was converted into a tea lounge and gift shop, and the staff was reduced to the bare minimum. Throughout the years, several paintings, antiques, and other objets d'art were sold, often at rock bottom rates, according to the children, while they described the way the house was restored' in disparaging terms. Earl Spencer consistently defended his wife's strong estate management, saying, 'The expense of restoration has been tremendous.'

However, Raine and his children's strained relationship was unmistakable throughout this time. She publicly commented on the schism when she told newspaper columnist Jean Rook, 'I'm utterly sick of the "Wicked Stepmother" lark. You'll never make me sound like a human being since people assume I'm Dracula's mother, but I did have a bad start and things are only getting better now. Sarah despised me, even my position at the head of the table, and issued orders to the servants above my head. Jane did not talk to me for two years, even if we met in a passageway. Diana was kind and always did her own thing.

Diana's rage toward Raine had been simmering for years before it erupted in 1989 at the church rehearsal for her brother's wedding to Victoria Lockwood, a prominent model. Raine refused to talk to Diana's mother at church, despite the fact that they were sitting in the same pew. Diana released all of her problems, which had been building up inside her for over 10 years. When Diana challenged her, Raine answered, 'You have no idea how much anguish your mother caused your father.' Diana, who subsequently claimed that she had never been so furious, turned on her stepmother. 'Pain, Raine, is a word you can't even relate to. In my work and role, I witness people suffering in ways you will never see, and you call it pain. You have a lot to learn. There was plenty more in the same vein. Afterward, her mother stated that it was the first time anyone in the family had defended her.

However, in the early days of Raine's time at Althorp, the youngsters dismissed her as a joke. They capitalised on her proclivity for categorising home guests into proper social groups. When Charles returned from Eton, where he was then attending school, he had prepared his pals to give phoney names. So one boy introduced himself as 'James Rothschild', hinting that he was a member of the well-known financial family. Raine brightened. 'Oh, are you Hannah's son?' she inquired. Charles' schoolfriend admitted that he didn't know before compounding his error by spelling the surname erroneously in the visitors' register.

At a weekend cookout, one of Sarah's friends bet £100 that Charles could not hurl his stepmother into the swimming pool. Raine, who wore a ballgown to the shorts and T-shirt party, accepted Charles' invitation for a poolside dance. As he prepared for a judo throw, she recognized what was going on and slid away. Christmas in Althorp, directed by Raine Spencer, was a weird comedy in stark contrast to the extravagances of Park House. She ruled over the present opening like a strict timekeeper. The youngsters could only open the present she indicated after she checked her watch and gave the go-ahead to take the paper off. 'It was really insane,' Charles said.

The only bright point was Diana's decision to give one of her presents to a particularly irritable night-watchman. Diana intuitively realised that, despite his terrifying image, he was simply lonely. She and her brother visited him, and he was so moved by her gesture that he burst into tears. It was an early example of her sensitivity to the needs of others, which was observed by her headmistress, Miss Rudge, who gave her the Miss Clark Lawrence Award for contribution to the school during her last term in 1977.

Diana's self-confidence was developing, and her promotion to school prefect reflected this. Diana, like her sister Sarah, departed West Heath to attend the Institut Alpin Videmanette, an expensive finishing school near Gstaad in Switzerland, where she studied domestic science, dressmaking, and cooking. She was meant to speak just French all day. In fact, she and her buddy Sophie Kimball spoke English all the time, and the only thing she practised was her skiing. Diana was unhappy and constrained by the routine, and she was ready to get away. She wrote numerous letters asking her parents to bring her home. They finally gave up when she pointed out that they were merely squandering their money.

Diana felt as if a heavy weight had been lifted off her shoulders now that school was over. She visibly improved, becoming happier, livelier, and prettier. Diana appeared more mature and calm, and her sisters' friends looked at her with fresh eyes. Despite being shy and overweight, she was gaining popularity. 'She was wonderful, fun, charming, and kind,' according to a friend.

Sarah, on the other hand, was filled with jealousy as she watched Diana develop. London was her realm, and she did not want her sister to steal the spotlight from her. The crisis occurred on one of the last traditional weekends at Althorp. Diana asked her sister for a lift to London. Sarah disagreed, claiming that having an extra person in the car would be too expensive in terms of petrol. Her friends mocked her, realising for the first time that the balance in their relationship had moved in favour of cute Diana.

Diana had had enough of being her family's Cinderella. She had felt her spirit crushed by school routine and her character constrained by her minor status in the household. Diana was excited to spread her wings and begin her own life in London. The excitement of independence beckoned. Her brother Charles stated, "Suddenly the insignificant ugly duckling was obviously going to be a swan."

CHAPTER 3
'Such Hope in My Heart'

THE QUEST for the gorgeous prince was completed. He had found his gorgeous damsel, and the world had a fairytale. Cinderella was unhappy in her ivory tower, which isolated her from her friends, family, and the rest of the world. As the public rejoiced over the Prince's money, the shades of the prison house closed inexorably around Diana. Despite her aristocratic upbringing, this naïve young kindergarten teacher felt completely at sea in the deferential hierarchy of Buckingham Palace. Many tears were shed throughout those three months, and many more to follow. Weight simply slid off her waist, which went from 29 inches when the engagement was revealed to 231/2 inches on her wedding day. During this stressful time, she developed bulimia nervosa, which would take nearly a decade to conquer. Diana's note to her pals at Coleherne Court, which read, 'For God's sake, ring me up - I'm going to need you,' proved brutally accurate. Her friend Carolyn Bartholomew, who observed her deteriorate during her engagement, recalled: "She went to live at Buckingham Palace, and then the tears started." This little thing grew so skinny. I was very worried about her. She wasn't happy; she was suddenly thrust into all of this pressure, which was a nightmare for her. She was disoriented, assailed from all sides. It was a whirlwind, and she was ashen, grey. Her first night at Clarence House, the Queen Mother's London home, was the quiet before the storm. When she arrived, she was left to her own devices; no one from the royal family, least of all her future husband, felt it necessary to welcome her to her new environment. The popular myth depicts the Queen Mother clucking over Diana as she taught her the finer points of royal protocol, while the Queen's senior lady-in-waiting, Lady Susan Hussey, took the young woman aside for regal history lessons. In actuality, Diana had less training for her new job than the average supermarket checkout operator.

Diana was shown to her first-floor bedroom by a servant. There was a note on her bed. It came from Camilla Parker Bowles and was written a few days before the engagement was publicly confirmed. The polite note asked her for a meal. Diana became suspicious during the encounter, which had been scheduled to coincide with Prince Charles' tour to Australia and New Zealand. Camilla repeatedly asked Diana if she planned to hunt when she relocated to Highgrove. Diana was perplexed by such an unusual inquiry and responded negatively. Camilla's expression of relief was apparent. Diana eventually discovered that Camilla regarded Charles' passion for hunting as a way to maintain her own friendship. It was unclear at the moment. Then again, nothing was. Diana quickly moved into apartments at Buckingham Palace, where she, her mother, and a small crew had to plan her wedding and outfit. Diana immediately realised that the royal family simply likes to alter their outfits. With the year split into three official seasons and frequently requiring four formal changes of clothing per day, her wardrobe of one long dress, one silk shirt, and a smart pair of shoes was completely inadequate. During her courtship, she would frequently raid her friends' clothes to ensure that she had suitable clothing to go out in. While her mother assisted her in selecting the renowned blue engagement suit she purchased from Harrods, she sought assistance from her sisters' friend Anna Harvey, Vogue magazine's fashion editor, on how to assemble her formal wardrobe. She realised that her working attire had to be not only fashionable, but also able to withstand the rigours of walkabouts, the intrusion of photographers, and her constant adversary, the wind. She progressively learned secrets of the profession, such as weighing her hems to keep them from blowing up in a breeze, and she amassed a circle of designers that included Catherine Walker, David Sassoon, and Victor Edelstein. Initially, there was no big plan; it was simply a matter of choosing who was available or who had been recommended by her new Vogue acquaintances. She chose two young designers, David and Elizabeth Emanuel, to create the wedding gown after being inspired by their work during a photo shoot at Lord Snowdon's Kensington studio. They also constructed the evening gown for her first formal engagement, a charity event in London, which was almost as well-received as the outfit she wore to St Paul's Cathedral a few months later. The strapless and backless black taffeta silk ball gown featured a plunging décolletage that defied gravity. Prince Charles was not thrilled by the attire. While she thought black was the smartest hue a girl her age could wear, he had a different opinion. When she came in her finery at the entrance of his study, he made an unfavourable comment, claiming that only mourners wore black. Diana said that she was not yet a part of his family and that she had no other clothes appropriate for the occasion. That spat did little to boost her confidence as she confronted a swarm of cameras waiting outside Goldsmiths Hall. She had never been taught the finer points of royal protocol and was frightened of embarrassing her fiancé in some manner. 'It was a horrific event,' she informed her friends. During the evening, she met Princess Grace of Monaco, a figure she had long admired from afar. She spotted Diana's uneasiness and rushed her away to the powder room, disregarding the other guests who were still talking about Diana's outfit choice. Diana opened out about the publicity, her feelings of loneliness, and her anxieties for the future. 'Don't worry,' Princess Grace quipped. 'It will get much worse.'

At the close of the historic month of March, Prince Charles headed to Australia for a five-week stay. Before climbing the gangway of the RAF VC10, he grabbed her arm and kissed each cheek. As she saw his plane taxi away, she burst into tears. Her vulnerability made her more appealing to the people. However, her tears were not as they appeared. Before leaving for the airport, he finished off a few last-minute items in his study at Buckingham Palace. Diana was conversing with him when the phone rang. It was Camilla. Diana debated whether to sit there or go and let them say their goodbyes in privacy. She left her fiancé alone, but later told friends that the incident crushed her heart. She was alone in the ivory tower. Buckingham Palace felt foreign to a girl accustomed to the loudness and turmoil of an all-girls apartment. Diana considered it a place of 'dead energy' and grew to loathe the suave evasions and subtle equivocations used by courtiers, especially when she asked them directly about her fiancé's previous relationship with Camilla Parker Bowles. Lonely and depressed, she frequently travelled from her second-floor flat to the kitchens to chat with the staff. On one legendary occasion, Diana, barefoot and simply clad in denim, buttered bread for an amazed footman. She found consolation in her passion of dancing, inviting the West Heath School pianist, Lily Snipp, and her dance teacher, Wendy Mitchell, to Buckingham Palace for individual lessons. Diana, clothed in a black leotard, performed a 40-minute ballet and tap dance routine. During those pivotal days, Miss Snipp kept a diary, which provided a firsthand account of Lady Diana Spencer's concerns as the wedding date approached. The first item in Miss Snipp's diary, on Friday, June 5, 1981, detailed Diana's first lesson. She wrote, "To Buckingham Palace to play for Lady Diana." We all worked hard during the lecture, with no time wasted. When the lecture was finished, Lady Diana, tongue in cheek, said, "I suppose Miss Snipp will now go directly to Fleet Street." She has a good sense of humour; she will need it in the coming years.

The most painful lecture, which turned out to be the last, was given a few days before the wedding. Diana's thoughts were focused on the momentous changes that lay ahead. Miss Snipp remarked that Lady Diana was fatigued from too many late nights. I delivered lovely silver salt-cellars as a gift from West Heath School, which were well liked. Lady Diana is counting down the number of days she has left to be free. That's quite depressing. Massive crowds gathered outside the Palace. We expect to resume lessons in October. Lady Diana stated, "In 12 days time, I shall no longer be me."

Diana must have realised as she spoke those comments that she had abandoned her bachelor character as soon as she stepped through the Palace portals. In the weeks after the engagement, she gained confidence and self-assurance, with her sense of humour frequently rising to the surface. Lucinda Craig Harvey met her former cleaning lady numerous times throughout her engagement, including once at her brother-in-law Neil McCorquodale's 30th birthday celebration. 'She had a distance to her, and everyone was in awe of her,' she said. James Gilbey had also recognized this trait. She has always been regarded as a typical Sloane Ranger. That is not true. She was usually detached, determined, and matter-of-fact, bordering on dogmatic. That characteristic has now grown into an enormous presence.

While she was awestruck by Prince Charles and deferred to his every choice, she did not appear to be overwhelmed by the circumstances. She may have been frightened on the inside, but on the outside, she appeared cool, comfortable, and eager to have fun. She seemed at ease in the company of her pals at Prince Andrew's 21st birthday party at Windsor Castle. When her future brother-in-law asked where he could find the Duchess of Westminster, the wife of Britain's wealthiest nobleman, she quipped, 'Oh Andrew, do quit name dropping.' Her facial repartee, which was biting but not cruel, reminded her of her elder sister Sarah, who was the Society circuit's queen bee.

"Don't look so serious; it's not working," Diana quipped when she introduced Adam Russell to the Queen, Prince Charles, and other members of the royal family in the receiving line at the Buckingham Palace ball two days before her wedding. She appeared to be in excellent spirits and relaxed in her beautiful surroundings. There was no indication that a few hours earlier, she had collapsed in tears and really considered calling the whole thing off. The emotions were caused by the delivery of a parcel a few days earlier at the bustling Buckingham Palace office, which she shared with Michael Colbourne, who was then in charge of the Prince's finances, and several others. Diana insisted on unlocking it, despite strong objections from the Prince's right-hand man. The inside contained a gold chain bracelet with a blue enamel disc and the initials 'F' and 'G' interlaced. The initials signify for Camilla and Charles' nicknames, 'Fred' and 'Gladys', which Diana had learned about from acquaintances. It had hit home for her earlier when she discovered that the Prince had given Camilla a bouquet of flowers when she was unwell. He had once again utilised that nickname.

Work at the Prince's office at Buckingham Palace came to a standstill when Diana questioned her future husband about his suggested present. Despite her passionate and tearful protests, Charles insisted on presenting the symbol to the woman who had haunted their courting and would later cast a long shadow over their marriage. When she went to a rehearsal at St Paul's Cathedral two days before the wedding, she realised how big the deception was. The moment the camera lights came on, it ignited the churning feelings in her heart, and she broke down and wept uncontrollably. Her irritation and desperation were on full display the weekend before the wedding, when she burst into tears on a polo field at Tidworth. By then, however, the television cameras were set up for the wedding, the cake had been cooked, the crowds were already forming on the street, and the excitement was almost palpable. Diana seriously considered putting off her wedding on the Monday before it took place. At lunchtime, she discovered that Prince Charles had gone to present Camilla with her gift, leaving behind his top security, Chief Inspector John McLean. Diana had lunch with her sisters at Buckingham Palace while Harry was meeting Camilla, and they discussed her position. She was perplexed, upset, and baffled by the sequence of events. They mocked her anxieties and forebodings about the impending calamity as she was seriously considering cancelling the wedding. 'Bad luck, Duch,' they added, using the family nickname for their younger sister, 'your face is on the tea-towels so you're too late to duck out.'

Her mind and heart were in turmoil, but no one would have expected it when she and Charles hosted a ball inside Buckingham Palace for 800 of their friends and family later that evening. It was a wonderful night of uproarious fun. Princess Margaret fastened a balloon to her tiara, Prince Andrew tied another to the tails of his dinner jacket, and royal bartenders served a beverage labelled 'A Long Slow Comfortable Screw up against the Throne'. Rory Scott remembers dancing with Diana in front of Margaret Thatcher, the then-Prime Minister, and embarrassed himself by constantly stepping on her toes. The comedian Spike Milligan spoke about God, Diana gave a priceless diamond and pearl necklace to a friend to look after while she danced, and the Queen was seen looking through the program and saying in bemused tones, 'It says here they have live music', as if it had just been invented. Diana's brother, Charles, who lived just down the road from Eton, recalls bowing to one of the servers. 'He was absolutely laden down with medals,' he remembered, 'and by that moment, with so many royals present, I was in automatic bowing mode. I bowed, and he seemed shocked. Then he asked if I wanted a drink. Most of the attendees spent the evening in a state of pleasure. 'It was an intoxicatingly cheerful environment,' said Adam Russell. "Everyone was horribly drunk and then catching taxis in the early hours; it was a glorious, happy blur."

Diana's attitude was greatly improved on the eve of the wedding, which she spent at Clarence House, when Charles brought her a signet ring engraved with the Prince of Wales feathers and an emotional message that read: 'I'm so proud of you, and when you come up, I'll be there at the altar for you tomorrow. "Just look them in the eye and knock 'em dead."

While his compassionate note helped to alleviate her concerns, it was difficult to contain the internal anguish that had been building up over the months. She ate everything she could that evening at dinner with her sister Jane before becoming ill. The stress and strain of the occasion contributed to the episode, but it was also an early indicator of bulimia nervosa, an illness that would take root later that year. She later admitted: "The night before the wedding, I was very, very calm, deathly calm." I felt like a lamb to be slaughtered. I knew it, but I couldn't do anything about it. She awoke early on the morning of July 29, 1981, which was not surprising given that her room overlooked the Mall, where the singing, chattering masses had been gathered for days. It was the beginning of what she later characterised as 'the most emotionally difficult day of my life'. Listening to the crowds outside, she sensed a deathly calm mixed with immense eagerness for the event that lay ahead. Her hairstylist, Kevin Shanley, make-up artist Barbara Daly, and David and Elizabeth Emanuel were all present to ensure that the bride looked her best. They succeeded. Her brother, Charles, recalls his sister's metamorphosis. 'She was never one for makeup, but she looked great. It was the first time in my life that I thought Diana was attractive. She looked gorgeous and serene that day, with no signs of anxiety despite her slightly pale complexion. She was joyful and serene. Her father, who gave her away, was ecstatic. "Darling, I'm so proud of you," he murmured as she walked down the staircase at Clarence House. Diana faced a number of practical challenges as she climbed into the Glass Coach with her father. Her dressmakers realised too late that they had not considered the coach's dimensions when designing the ivory silk wedding gown with its 25-foot-long train. Despite Diana's best attempts, it was severely crushed during the short voyage to St Paul's. She also knew it was her priority to get her father, who had been physically disabled since his stroke, down the long aisle. 'It was a profoundly poignant moment for us when he created it,' Charles Spencer said. Earl Spencer enjoyed the carriage trip and waved passionately to the spectators. As they approached St Martin-in-the-Fields Church, the cheering was so loud that he assumed they had arrived at St Paul's and prepared to exit the carriage. When they arrived at the cathedral, the entire world held its breath as Diana, her father leaning heavily on her arm, walked painfully slowly down the aisle. Diana had plenty of time to spot the guests, including Camilla Parker Bowles. As she walked down the aisle, her heart overflowed with love and admiration for Charlie. When she stared at him through her veil, her fears were gone, and she felt like the luckiest girl in the world. She had so much hope for the future, knowing that he would love, nurture, and protect her from the challenges that were ahead. 750 million people in over 70 countries witnessed that event on television. The Archbishop of Canterbury described it as 'the stuff on which fairytales are formed'.

But for the time being, she had to focus on dipping a formal curtsy to the Queen, a thought that had preoccupied her for several days. When the newly formed Princess of Wales emerged from St Paul's Cathedral to the crowd's cheers, her heart was filled with hope and gladness. She told herself that the bulimia that had ruined her engagement was just a case of pre-wedding anxiety, and Mrs Parker Bowles was history. She later spoke of those heady emotions with ironic amusement: 'I had huge dreams in my heart.'

She was proven quite wrong. Prince Charles and Camilla's bond continues to this day. In Diana's mind, this impossible triangle caused a decade of anxiety, anguish, and wrath. There were no winners. Diana put it succinctly: 'There were three of us in this marriage, so it was a bit crowded.' A friend of both of them, who witnessed the terrible drama unfold over the next decade, admitted: "I am sorry for the tragedy of it all." My heart hurts for everyone involved in this misunderstanding, but especially for Diana. However, on that July day, Diana basked in the warm affection of the public who lined the way back to Buckingham Palace, where the royal family and their guests had the usual royal wedding breakfast. By then, she was simply too tired to think straight, and the patriotic crowd's spontaneous expression of devotion had completely overwhelmed her. She longed for peace and privacy, hoping that now that the wedding was done, she would return to relative obscurity. The royal couple sought privacy at Broadlands, Earl Mountbatten's Hampshire residence, where they spent the first three days of their honeymoon, followed by a leisurely Mediterranean trip aboard the royal yacht Britannia, which they boarded in Gibraltar. Prince Charles has his own views about marital life. He packed along his fishing gear from their Hampshire retreat, as well as a half-dozen novels by his friend and mentor, South African philosopher and adventurer Sir Laurens Van der Post. It was his idea that they read his books together and then discuss van der Post's mystical notions over meals. Diana, on the other hand, wanted to spend quality time with her husband. For much of their engagement, his royal duties kept him away from her side. On board the royal vessel, which had 21 officers and 256 men, they were never left alone. Evening meals were black tie affairs attended by a select group of officials. While they talked about the day's events, a Royal Marine band played in an adjacent room. The royal couple was exhausted from the intense strain surrounding the wedding. They slept a lot, and Diana spent a lot of time in the kitchens, which were run by 'Swampy' Marsh and his colleagues. They were charmed by her insatiable appetite for ice cream and her requests for special snacks in between meals. Diana's hunger perplexed royal servants and acquaintances throughout the years, especially given her slender figure. She was frequently spotted raiding the refrigerator at Highgrove late at night, and she even astonished a footman by devouring a whole steak and kidney pie when vacationing at Windsor Castle. Her friend Rory Scott recalls her eating a 1lb bag of sweets in quick succession during a bridge session, and her admission that she ate a bowl of custard before going to bed adding to the mystery surrounding her diet.

In truth, Diana suffered from bulimia nervosa almost from the moment she became Princess of Wales, which explains her unpredictable dietary habits. Carolyn Bartholomew, who was key in getting Diana to seek medical attention, stated, 'It's been there throughout her royal career, without a question. I hate to say it, but I believe it may emerge when she is under pressure. According to the Consumers' Association's most current Drug and Therapeutics report, approximately 2% of young women in Britain suffer from bulimia. These ladies engage in episodes of enormous overeating accompanied by a sensation of loss of control. Between eating episodes, most victims fast or vomit. Binges are typically secretive, sometimes pre-planned, and are frequently followed by severe mood fluctuations manifested as guilt, sadness, self-hatred, and even suicidal behaviour. Sufferers typically have a normal body weight but perceive themselves to be overweight, bloated, and ugly. This hatred for their bodies leads to fasting in between periods of overeating, and sufferers frequently experience feelings of failure, low self-esteem, and lack of control. Long-term bulimia can cause muscle cramping, kidney problems, and even heart failure.

Bulimia, unlike anorexia nervosa, persists through disguise. It is a sophisticated illness in the sense that sufferers refuse to admit they have a problem. They constantly look to be joyful and dedicate their lives to helping others. However, there is hatred beneath the cheerful grin, anger that sufferers are unwilling to express. Women in caring occupations, such as nursing and nannying, are especially vulnerable to the condition. They perceive their own wants as avarice and hence feel guilty about caring for themselves. That revulsion is turned into intense purging via vomiting or laxatives. According to the medical advisory, bulimia nervosa is a dangerous, underrecognized, potentially chronic, and possibly fatal condition that affects many young women but rarely men.

While the roots of bulimia and anorexia can be traced back to childhood and a dysfunctional family history, uncertainty and worry in adulthood serve as the trigger for the condition. Diana's last few months had been an emotional rollercoaster as she struggled to cope with her new life as a public person, the smothering publicity, and her husband's unclear behaviour toward her. It was an explosive cocktail, and it only took one spark to start her disease. According to Diana, the week after they were engaged, Charles put his arm around her waist and made a joke about her chubbiness. It was a harmless comment, yet it stirred something within her. She then got herself sick. It was a powerful release of tension that offered her a sense of control over herself as well as an opportunity to express her rage.

Their honeymoon provided little respite. Diana made herself sick four, if not five, times every day, making the situation considerably worse. Camilla's omnipresent shadow only added fuel to the fire. Reminders were everywhere. When they were comparing engagements in their journals, two images of Camilla slipped out of Charles' diary. Among the tears and angry words, she begged him to be honest about how he felt about her and Camilla. Those words didn't go through. Several days later, they entertained Egyptian President Anwar Sadat and his wife Jihan aboard the royal yacht. When Charles arrived for dinner, Diana saw he was wearing a new pair of cufflinks in the shape of two entwined 'C's. He confirmed they were from Camilla but dismissed them as a simple gesture of goodwill. Diana did not see it this way. She couldn't understand why Charles needed these continual reminders of Camilla, she told friends angrily.

Diana, on the other hand, seemed upbeat and cheerful in public. She got in on a singsong in the sailors' mess, playing 'What shall we do with a drunken sailor?' after drinking from a beer can. 'We were all tickled pink,' says one sailor. One moonlit night, they had a BBQ in a bay off the coast of Ithaca. The yacht's officers coordinated it, and they performed all of the cooking themselves. After everyone had dined, a Royal Marine accordionist arrived, song papers were distributed, and the night air was filled with the sounds of Boy Scout songs and sea shanties.

In its own way, the honeymoon conclusion was the highlight of the vacation. For days, the officers and troops had practised a farewell concert. There were over 14 performers, ranging from stand-up comedians to bawdy sing-alongs. The royal couple returned to Britain looking fit, tanned, and in love, and flew to join the Queen and the rest of the royal family at the Balmoral estate.

However, the Highland mists did little to calm Diana's disturbed spirit. Indeed, when they landed at Balmoral, where they resided from August to late October, the full influence of their life as Princess of Wales became apparent. She had anticipated, like many others in the royal family, that her renown would be fleeting, with her shine quickly dimming after the wedding. Everyone, including newspaper editors, was taken off guard by the Princess Diana phenomenon. Their readers couldn't get enough of Diana; her face appeared on every magazine cover, every facet of her life drew attention, and anybody who had ever met her was tracked down to be interviewed by the voracious media.

In less than a year, this insecure high school dropout had been deified by the press and public. Her daily actions, such as opening a car door for herself or purchasing a bag of sweets, were praised as proof of a very human princess. Everyone became ill, even the royal family's guests in Balmoral that autumn. Diana was in a state of tremendous confusion. She hadn't changed much in the past year since she was covering automobiles with eggs and flour and ringing doorbells with her giggling buddies.

As she mingled with the guests at the Queen's Scottish home, she realised that she was no longer treated as a person but as a position, no longer a flesh and blood human being with thoughts and feelings, but as a symbol, with the title 'Her Royal Highness, the Princess of Wales' separating her not only from the general public but also from those within the intimate royal circle. Protocol required that she be addressed as 'Your Royal Highness' on the first occasion and 'Ma'am' afterward. Of course, everyone curtsied. Diana was disconcerted. 'Don't call me ma'am, call me Duch,' she told a pal shortly after being married. But no matter how hard she tried, she couldn't stop the shift in perceptions about her.

She understood that everyone was looking at her with fresh eyes, treating her as if she were a valuable piece of porcelain to be appreciated but not touched. Diana was treated with kid gloves when all she required was some sound advice, an embrace, and a comforting word. However, the bewildered young lady who was the true Diana was in severe risk of drowning in the tidal surge of change that had turned her life upside-down. She grinned and laughed in front of everyone, as if she was overjoyed with her husband and newfound status. At a well-known photocall on the Bridge of Dee on the Balmoral estate, Diana informed the assembled journalists that she could 'highly encourage' marriage. However, away from the cameras and microphones, the pair clashed often. Diana was constantly on edge, suspecting Camilla's involvement in Charles' every move. At times, she thought he was asking Camilla for advice on his marriage or making plans to meet her. A close acquaintance stated, 'They had stunning rows about her, real stinkers, and I don't blame Diana one bit.'

She was torn between jealousy and profound devotion to Charles. Diana was still completely smitten with him, and Charles was, in his own way, in love with her. They went on lengthy walks across the hills that surround Balmoral, and as they lay in the heather, he read portions from works by the Swiss psychiatrist Carl Jung or Laurens van der Post. Charles was content, and Diana shared his happiness. The poignant love letters they exchanged spoke to their increasing tie of attachment.

However, these love interludes were merely interruptions in Diana's fears about public life, which did little to alleviate her bulimic condition. She was constantly unwell, and her weight dropped dramatically until she was literally skin and bone'. At this important point in her life, she felt she had no one she could confide in. She anticipated, correctly, that the Queen and other members of the royal family would support her husband. In any case, the royal family is trained and inclined to avoid emotional breast thumping. They live in a world of restrained emotions and controlled behaviour. They felt Diana would be able to quickly adopt their strict code of conduct.

She didn't even feel comfortable approaching her own family for help. Her parents and sisters were sympathetic, but they wanted her to stick to the status quo. Her companions, particularly her previous flatmates, would have rallied behind her, but she didn't want to burden them with such responsibility. She understood that, like the rest of the world, they wanted the royal story to succeed. They believed the myth, and Diana couldn't bring herself to tell them the terrible truth. She was extremely alone and exposed. Her thoughts inevitably turned to suicide, not because she wanted to die, but because she badly needed help. Her husband took matters into his own hands, inviting Laurens van der Post to travel to Scotland to see what he might accomplish. His interventions proved ineffective, so she flew to London in early October for professional counselling. She met with numerous doctors and psychologists at Buckingham Palace. They prescribed different tranquillisers to help her calm down and regain her equilibrium. Diana, on the other hand, resolutely rejected their advice. She understood in her heart that she didn't need medications; instead, she needed rest, compassion, and understanding from those around her. She learned she was pregnant while being besieged by voices pressuring her to accept the physicians' suggestions. 'Thank Heavens for William,' she later remarked, because it meant she could now legitimately refuse the drugs she was offered, claiming she did not want to risk physical or mental deformity in the baby she was carrying. Her pregnancy provided a reprieve. The reprieve would not last long.

CHAPTER 4
'My Cries for Help'

The sound of angry voices and frantic sobbing could be heard clearly from the Prince and Princess of Wales' suite of rooms at Sandringham House. It was shortly after Christmas, but there was little holiday spirit between the royal couple. Diana was three months pregnant with Prince William and felt completely miserable. Her relationship with Prince Charles was quickly deteriorating. The Prince seems unable or unwilling to comprehend Diana's turmoil. She was suffering from terrible morning sickness, was tormented by Camilla Parker Bowles, and was urgently attempting to adjust to her new job and family. As she subsequently told friends, 'One minute I was a nobody, the next I was Princess of Wales, mother, media toy, member of this family, and it was just too much for one person to bear.' She had pleaded, cajoled, and quarrelled furiously in an attempt to earn the Prince's support. In vain. On that January day in 1982, her first New Year with the royal family, she threatened to kill herself. He accused her of lying and made plans to ride around the Sandringham estate. She was true to her word. Standing atop the wooden staircase, she threw herself to the ground, landing in a heap at the bottom. The Queen was among the first to arrive on the scene. She was shocked, literally shivering from the shock of what she had seen. A local doctor was summoned, while Diana's gynaecologist, George Pinker, travelled from London to see his royal patient. Her husband simply rejected her suffering and continued with his plans to go riding. Fortunately, Diana was not gravely injured by the fall, but she did get severe bruising around her midsection. A thorough examination confirmed that the foetus had not been damaged. The event was one of several home crises that engulfed the royal couple during those turbulent early days. At each turning point, they increased their distance from one another. Her friend James Gilbey described her suicide attempts as "messages of complete desperation." Please assist. Diana attempted suicide and made repeated threats throughout their early marriage. It should be noted that these were not serious efforts to end her life, but rather calls for aid. On one occasion, she hurled herself into a glass display cabinet at Kensington Palace, and on another, she sliced her wrists with a razor. Another time, she cut herself with the serrated edge of a lemon slicer; on another occasion, following a furious disagreement with Prince Charles, she took up a penknife from his dressing table and sliced her breast and thighs. Despite her bleeding, her spouse scorned her. He assumed she was making up for her difficulties, like he often did. Later, her sister Jane, who saw her soon after, commented on the score marks on her body. Jane was terrified when she discovered the truth.

As Diana subsequently told friends, "They were desperate cries for help." I simply needed time to adjust to my new situation. One person who witnessed their relationship deteriorate refers to Prince Charles' apathy and complete lack of regard for Diana during a time when she really needed assistance. 'His coldness pushed her over the edge, although he might have romanced her until the end of the earth. They could have set the planet ablaze. He instilled hatred in herself through no fault of his own, as a result of his own ignorance, upbringing, and lack of a complete relationship with anyone in his life.

This is a partisan assessment. In the early days of their marriage, Prince Charles attempted to ease his wife into the royal routine. Her first major test was a three-day trip to Wales in October 1981. The spectators made it painfully clear who was the new star of the show: the Princess of Wales. Charles had to apologise for not having enough wives. If he took one side of the street during a walkabout, the audience grumbled because they had come to meet his wife. 'I seem to do nothing but collect flowers these days,' he admitted. 'I understand my role.' Other murmured concerns might be heard behind the smiling faces. The Princess's first appearance on a rainy quayside in Wales surprised royal observers. It was the first time I'd seen Diana up close since the extended honeymoon, and it felt like I was staring at a different lady. She was not just slim, but excruciatingly thin.

She had lost weight before the wedding, which was to be expected, but the girl moving through the people, shaking hands and taking flowers, appeared almost transparent. Diana was two months pregnant and felt worse than she looked. She dressed inappropriately for the pouring rain that followed them everywhere, was plagued by severe morning sickness, and was completely overwhelmed by the masses who had gathered to see her. Diana stated that she was difficult to control throughout the baptism of fire. She was frequently in tears as they travelled to the various sites, telling her husband that she couldn't handle the crowds. She lacked the energy and resources to deal with the thought of meeting so many people. There were numerous times when she wished she could return to her safe bachelor flat with her happy, straightforward companions.

While Prince Charles sympathised with his grieving wife, he demanded that the royal roadshow continue. He was naturally nervous when Diana delivered her first speech, partially in Welsh, at Cardiff City Hall when she was honoured with the Freedom of the City. Diana easily passed that exam, but she also found another truism about royal life. Regardless of how brilliantly she performed or how hard she tried, she received no recognition from her husband, the royal family, or their courtiers. In her fragile, lonely situation, a little praise would have been really beneficial. 'I remember her stating that she was working so hard and all she needed was a pat on the back,' said a pal. 'But it was not forthcoming.' Every day, she battled illness to keep her public appearances on schedule. She had such a neurotic fear of disappointing her husband and the royal family 'firm' that she carried out her formal duties despite being plainly ill. On two occasions, she had to cancel commitments; on others, she appeared pale and ill, acutely conscious that she was not assisting her husband. At least when her pregnancy was formally confirmed on November 5, 1981, Diana was able to discuss it publicly. The exhausted Princess explained, 'Some days I felt dreadful. Nobody informed me I would feel the way I did. She confessed to a love of bacon and tomato sandwiches and called her friend, Sarah Ferguson, the daughter of Charles' polo manager, Major Ronald Ferguson. The exuberant redhead would frequently leave her job at a London art dealer and drive to Buckingham Palace to cheer up the royal mother-to-be.

In private, things were no better. She steadfastly refused to take any medicines, stating once more that she could not hold herself accountable if the baby was born malformed. At the same time, she admitted that the rest of the royal family regarded her as 'a problem'. At formal dinners at Sandringham or Windsor Castle, she regularly had to leave the table due to illness. Instead of simply going to bed, she insisted on returning, believing it was her responsibility to try to meet her duties. If daily living was challenging, public duties were unbearable. The trip to Wales had been a success, but Diana had been overwhelmed by her popularity, the size of the crowds, and the proximity of the media. She was riding a tiger and there was no way out. For the first several months, she was frightened at the prospect of performing an official engagement alone. Wherever feasible, she would accompany Charles and stay by his side, silent, attentive, but afraid. When she accepted her first single public duty, turning on the Christmas lights on Regent Street in London's West End, she was gripped with fear. She felt nauseous while giving a brief speech in a hurried monotone. After that engagement, she was relieved to return home to Buckingham Palace. It did not get any easier. The girl who would only appear in school plays as a non-speaking character was now centre stage. According to her own admission, it took her six years to feel comfortable in her main role. Luckily for her, the camera had already fallen for the new royal cover girl. Regardless of how nervous she was on the inside, her welcoming grin and unpretentious demeanour made a photographer's day. For once, the camera did lie, not about her beauty, but about concealing the sensitive personality beneath her seamless ability to enchant. She believed that her ability to grin despite suffering was due to attributes inherited from her mother. When friends wondered how she maintained such cheerful public demeanour, she said, "I have what my mother has." Regardless of how bloody you are, you can put up the most magnificent display of happiness. My mother is an expert at this, and I've picked it up. It kept the wolves away from the door.

The capacity to adopt this happy persona in public was aided by the nature of bulimia, which is a disorder in which sufferers can retain their normal body weight, as opposed to its sister illness, anorexia nervosa, in which sufferers thin to skin and bone. Diana's healthy lifestyle, which included regular exercise, limited alcohol, and early nights, also provided her with the energy she needed to carry out her royal duties. According to an eating disorders expert, bulimics refuse to recognize they have a problem. They are always smiling, have no troubles in their lives, and spend their time attempting to please others. But there is misery underneath because they are afraid to voice their displeasure. At the same time, her strong sense of duty and obligation drove her to maintain appearances for the sake of the public. A close acquaintance stated, "The public side of her was very different from the private side." They wanted a fairy princess to come and touch them, transforming everything into gold. All of their troubles will be forgotten. They had no idea the person was crucifying herself internally. Diana, an unwilling international media celebrity, was forced to learn on the go. There was no training, support, or counsel from within the royal system. Everything was fragmented and unplanned. Charles' courtiers were accustomed to dealing with a bachelor with strict habits and a defined regimen. Marriage changed everything. During the wedding preparations, there was concern that Prince Charles might be unable to afford his portion of the costs. 'Sums were worked up on the backs of envelopes; it was mayhem,' said a former member of his Household. The momentum that lasted long after the ceremony surprised everyone. Even though more workers were brought in, Diana sat down to respond to many of the 47,000 messages of congratulations and 10,000 gifts that the wedding generated. She constantly had to pinch herself due to the ridiculousness of the situation. She went from scrubbing floors for a living to receiving a pair of brass candlesticks from the King and Queen of Sweden or making small chats with the President of Somewhere or Other. Fortunately, her upbringing had equipped her with the social skills necessary to deal with these situations. This was a good thing because the royal family's federal structure requires everyone to stay inside their province.

In addition to adjusting to her public role, the young princess needed to furnish and decorate two houses. Prince Charles appreciated her sense of style and colour and delegated the task of decorating to her. However, she did require expert assistance. She appreciated her mother's recommendation of Dudley Poplak, a modest South African-born interior designer who had decorated her own residences. He began work on Apartments Eight and Nine at Kensington Palace and Highgrove. His primary responsibility was to fit as many wedding gifts into their new homes as possible. The royal couple received an 18th-century travelling commode from the Duke and Duchess of Wellington, a pair of Georgian chairs from the people of Bermuda, and wrought-iron gates from the neighbouring community of Tetbury, to name a few of the many gifts. For long of her pregnancy, Diana remained at Buckingham Palace as painters and carpenters worked on their new London residence. The royal couple did not move into Kensington Palace until five weeks before

Prince William's birth, when they also lived with Princess Margaret, the Duke and Duchess of Gloucester, and their close neighbours, Prince and Princess Michael of Kent. Diana was really exhausted by this point. She was continuously watched by photographers and reporters, and newspapers reported on her every move. Unknown to the Princess, the Queen had previously summoned Fleet Street newspaper editors to Buckingham Palace, where her press secretary asked for Diana's privacy. The request was ignored. When Charles and Diana flew to Windermere Island in the Bahamas in February, two tabloid media representatives accompanied them. The Princess, who was five months pregnant at the time, was photographed sprinting through the surf in a bikini. She and Charles were outraged by the photos' publication, and the Palace observed that it was one of 'the blackest days in British media'. The honeymoon between the press, the Princess, and the Palace practically ended. This everyday media infatuation with Diana strained her already overworked mental and physical energies. Her bulimia, morning sickness, failing marriage, and jealousy of Camilla combined to make her life unbearable. The media's curiosity in the upcoming delivery was simply too much to bear. She chose to have the labour induced despite the fact that her gynaecologist, George Pinker, stated, 'Birth is a natural process and should be treated as such.' While she was acutely aware of her mother's distress during the birth of her brother John, her intuition assured her that the baby was fine. 'It's well cooked,' she informed a pal before accompanying Prince Charles to the private Lindo wing of St Mary's Hospital in Paddington, west London. Her labour, like her pregnancy, seemed to go forever and was extremely tough. Diana was frequently ill, and Mr Pinker and his colleagues contemplated doing an emergency Caesarean procedure. Diana's fever rose substantially during her birth, raising concerns about the baby's health. Diana, who had an epidural injection at the base of her spine, was eventually able to give birth on her own, without the use of forceps or surgery.

Joy was unconfined. Diana gave birth to her son and heir on June 21, 1982, at 9.03 p.m., which sparked national celebration. When the Queen came to see her grandchild the next day, her reaction was usual. As she glanced at the little bundle, she commented drily, "Thank goodness he doesn't have ears like his father." The second in line to the throne was still officially known as 'Baby Wales,' and it took the couple many days of deliberation before they settled on a name. Prince Charles stated as much: 'We've considered one or two. There's some debate over it, but we'll find an answer eventually. Charles intended to name his first son 'Arthur' and his second 'Albert' after Queen Victoria's consort. Diana chose William and Harry, while her husband's tastes were reflected in their children's middle names.

When the time came, Mom was equally firm about the boys' education. Prince Charles advocated that they should be raised first by his childhood nanny, Mabel Anderson, and subsequently by a governess who would teach the boys in the privacy of Kensington Palace for the first several years. This was how Prince Charles had been raised, and he expected his sons to follow suit. Diana advised that her children go to school alongside other children. She believed that her children should grow up in the real world rather than in the artificial atmosphere of a royal palace. Within the restrictions of the royal schedule, Diana tried to raise her children as normally as possible. Her own youth provided ample proof of the emotional trauma that can result when a child is handed from one parental figure to another. She was adamant that her children would never go without the embraces and kisses that she and her brother Charles wanted as children. While Barbara Barnes, the nanny for Lord and Lady Glenconner's children, was hired, it was made clear that Diana would be heavily involved in their development. Initially, she breastfed the boys, which she discussed incessantly with her sister Sarah. For a while, the joy of parenthood overpowered her eating disorder. Carolyn Bartholomew, who visited her at Kensington Palace three days after William was born, recalled: "She was overjoyed with both herself and the baby." She seemed content. The vibe was contagious. Charles once shocked his friends with his enthusiasm for the nursery routine. 'I was hoping to do some digging,' he told Harold Haywood, the Prince's Trust secretary, on Friday evening. But the ground is so hard that I can't get my spade in. So I anticipate changing nappies instead. As William matured, reports circulated about the Prince joining his son in the bath, William flushing his shoes down the lavatory, and Charles cutting short engagements to spend time with his family. There were also darker stories, such as Diana suffering from anorexia nervosa, Prince Charles being anxious about her health, and her exerting too much influence on his friends and staff. In actuality, the Princess suffered from both bulimia and severe postpartum depression. The preceding year's events had left her mentally fatigued, as well as physically exhausted from her chronic condition. The birth of William, and the subsequent psychological reaction, reignited the dark thoughts she had regarding her husband's closeness with Camilla Parker Bowles. When he didn't arrive home on time, there were tears and panicked phone calls, as well as sleepless nights while he was abroad. A friend definitely recalls the Princess calling him in tears. Diana had accidentally overheard her husband conversing on his mobile phone while taking a bath. She was very upset when she heard him say, 'Whatever happens, I will always love you.'

She was weepy and nervous, worrying about her kid - 'Is he all right, Barbara?' she would ask her new nanny - and neglecting herself. It was a really lonely moment. Her relatives and friends were now on the periphery of her new existence. At the same time, she was aware that the royal family saw her as both a problem and a threat. They were genuinely concerned about Prince Charles' choice to give up shooting, as well as his vegetarian tendencies. The royal family was concerned about the future since they own extensive estates in Scotland and Norfolk, where hunting, shooting, and fishing are an important element of land management. Diana was held responsible for her husband's change of heart. It was a terrible misinterpretation of her situation. Diana felt powerless to control her husband's actions. Changes in his attire were one thing; significant changes to the conventional country code were something else entirely. In truth, Charles' highly renowned vegetarianism can be attributed to his former bodyguard, Paul Officer, who frequently debated the benefits of a non-meat diet with him on long vehicle rides. She was also starting to understand the lay of the land with her in-laws. During a heated disagreement with Diana, Charles clarified the royal family's attitude. He told her unequivocally that his father, the Duke of Edinburgh, had agreed that if his marriage did not work out after five years, he may resume his bachelor lifestyle. The fact that those sentiments, shouted in the heat of the moment, were true or false was irrelevant. They had the effect of keeping Diana on guard in all of her interactions with her in-laws. At Balmoral, her mood became even more sad. The weather did little to brighten her spirits. It rained nonstop, and when the Princess was photographed leaving the castle on route to London, the media assumed she was bored with the Queen's Highland retreat and wanted to go shopping. In truth, she returned to Kensington Palace to seek professional help for her severe depression. Over time, she saw a variety of psychotherapists and psychologists, each with a unique approach to her various challenges. Some recommended medicines, like they did when she was pregnant with William, while others attempted to investigate her psychology. One of the first to treat her was Dr. Alan McGlashan, a Jungian psychotherapist and friend of Laurens van der Post, who had consultation facilities near Kensington Palace. He was intrigued by her dreams and encouraged her to write them down before discussing any hidden messages they may carry. She later stated that she was not convinced by this method of treatment. As a result, he ended his trips. However, his association with the royal family did not end there; since then, he has addressed numerous confidential things with Prince Charles, who has paid regular visits to his surgery near Sloane Street.

Another doctor, David Mitchell, was more concerned with discussing and analysing Diana's talks with her husband. He came to see her every evening and asked her to retell the happenings of the day. She acknowledged candidly that their conversations were more about tears than words. Other professional counsellors saw the Princess. While they each had their own opinions and beliefs, Diana did not believe any of them came close to comprehending the genuine depth of the turmoil in her heart and mind.

On November 11, Diana's doctor, Michael Linnett, expressed his concern about her health to her former West Heath pianist, Lily Snipp. She wrote in her diary, "Diana looked very beautiful and very thin." (Her doctor wants her to gain weight; she has no appetite.) I inquired about Prince William; he slept 13 hours last night! She stated that she and Charles are devoted parents, and their son is lovely.'

Ironically, when she was at her lowest point, the tide of publicity turned against her. She was no longer the storybook Princess, but a royal shopaholic who spent a fortune on a never-ending supply of new clothing. Diana was held accountable for the constant stream of royal workers who had left their service over the preceding 18 months, and the Princess was accused of forcing Charles to quit his friends, change his eating habits, and his clothes. Even the Queen's press secretary referred to their relationship as 'rumbustious'. At a time when she was having suicidal thoughts, gossip columnist Nigel Dempster referred to her as 'a devil and a monster'. Diana took the critique seriously, despite the fact that it was a terrible imitation of the truth. Later, her brother unknowingly reinforced the notion that she hired and fired employees when he said, 'In a quiet way she has weeded out a lot of the hangers-on who surrounded Charles.' He was referring to the Prince's adoring friends, but it was construed as a remark on the frequent staff turnover at Kensington Palace and Highgrove. In actuality, Diana was trying to keep her head above water, let alone implement a dramatic management reorganisation plan. Nonetheless, she bore the responsibility for what the media joyfully dubbed "Malice at the Palace," referring to the Princess as "the mouse that roared." In a fit of frustration, she informed James Whitaker, "I want you to realise that I am not responsible for any sackings. I don't just dismiss folks. Her outburst followed the resignation of Edward Adeane, the Prince's private secretary and a family member who had guided the monarchy since George V's reign.

In fact, Diana got along well with Adeane, who introduced her to many of the women she accepted as ladies-in-waiting while she was an ardent matchmaker, constantly attempting to couple the difficult bachelor with unattached ladies. When the Prince's dedicated valet, Stephen Barry, who subsequently died of Aids, resigned, the blame was placed on Diana. She had expected as much when he told her about leaving as they watched the sun set over the Mediterranean during their honeymoon trip. He, like the Prince's detective John McLean and several other staff members who served the Prince throughout his bachelorhood, understood it was time to depart once he was safely married. So it proved. As she struggled to accept the realities of her marriage and royal life, Diana had periods in those early years when she felt she could cope and contribute positively to the royal family and the nation as a whole. The initial glimmerings came in sad circumstances. When Princess Grace of Monaco died in a vehicle accident in September 1982, she vowed to attend her burial. Diana felt a sense of gratitude to the woman who had been so nice to her on her first terrible public appearance 18 months prior, as well as empathy for someone who, like her, had entered the royal world from the outside. Initially, she expressed her intention to attend the burial with her husband. He was sceptical and informed her that she would need to get consent from the Queen's private secretary. She sent him a memo, the standard form of royal communication, but he responded negatively, claiming that it was impossible because she had only been doing the job for a short time. Diana was so passionate about the matter that she refused to take no for an answer. This time she wrote directly to the Queen, who had no objections to the request. It was her first solo foreign travel representing the royal family, and she returned home to great plaudits for her dignified demeanour throughout the emotionally fraught and at times mawkish funeral service. Other obstacles were on the horizon. Prince William was still crawling when the government asked them to visit Australia. The media was rife with controversy over Diana's decision to accompany Prince William on her first major overseas journey, defying the Queen. In truth, Malcolm Fraser, the Australian Prime Minister, played a key role in this decision. He wrote to the royal couple, expressing his understanding of the difficulties that young families face and inviting them to bring the Prince with them. Until that point, they were content to leave him behind for the scheduled four-week tour. Fraser's thoughtful gift allowed them to extend their tour to include a two-week journey to New Zealand. The Queen's approval was never sought. During his tour, William stayed at Woomargama, a 4,000-acre sheep farm in New South Wales, with nanny Barbara Barnes and many security personnel. While his parents could only spend time with him on rare occasions due to his rigorous schedule, Diana knew he was under the same sky. His being in the country provided a wonderful conversation starter during their interminable walks, and Diana especially enjoyed discussing his improvement.

Diana's patience was put to the utmost during that stay. There have been few other moments since then with such unrelenting passion. In a country of 17 million people, approximately one million travelled to see the Prince and Princess of Wales as they moved from city to city. The welcome was sometimes frenzy-like. In Brisbane, where 300,000 people were crammed into the city centre, hysteria reached a fever pitch of 95 degrees. There were numerous occasions where an unanticipated surge in the crowd may have resulted in disaster. No one in the royal entourage, including the Prince of Wales, has ever received such praise.

The first few days were difficult. She was jetlagged, worried, and suffering from bulimia. After her first engagement at the Alice Springs School of the Air, she and her lady-in-waiting, Anne Beckwith-Smith, consoled one another. Diana cried her eyes out behind closed doors, exhausted from her nervousness. She wanted William, she wanted to go home, and she wanted to be anyplace other than Alice Springs. Even Anne, a mature and practical 29-year-old, was upset. That first week was an ordeal. She had been tossed in the deep end, and it was a case of sink or swim. Diana drew on her inner strength and persevered.

While Diana relied on her husband for leadership and guidance, how the press and public reacted to the royal couple only served to widen a gap between them. The masses objected, as they did in Wales, when Prince Charles crossed to their side of the street during a walkabout. The Princess received the majority of the attention in the press, with Charles playing a supporting role. Later that year, they spent three weeks in Canada. A former member of his household remarked, "He never expected this kind of reaction." After all, he was Prince of Wales. When he got out of the car, people groaned. It harmed his dignity, and he naturally got jealous. In the end, it was like working for two pop stars. It was all incredibly sad, which is why they are now doing everything separately.

In public, Charles graciously accepted the changed status quo; in private, he blamed Diana. Naturally, she stated that she had never desired this praise, and was instead appalled by media attention. Indeed, for a woman suffering from a self-image-related ailment, seeing her happy visage on the cover of every newspaper and magazine did little to assist.

Ultimately, the triumph of that arduous journey represented a watershed moment in her royal career. She went out as a girl, but returned home as a woman. It was nothing like the transformation she would go through a few years later, but it foreshadowed the gradual resurrection of her inner spirit. For a long time, she had been out of control, unable to deal with the daily responsibilities of her new royal position. She now had the confidence and experience to perform in public. There were still tears and traumas, but the worst had passed. She slowly began to pick up the strands of her existence. For a long time, she had been unable to confront many of her friends. She realised that being imprisoned would make hearing news from her former circle painful. In their eyes, talking about their vacations, dinner parties, and new professions seemed insignificant in comparison to her newfound international fame. But for Diana, this conversation represented freedom, something she could no longer enjoy.

Diana didn't want her pals to see her in such a bad mood. She acted like an injured animal, seeking to lick her wounds in peace and privacy. Following her travels in Australia and Canada, she felt confident enough to rebuild her friendships and wrote several letters inquiring about everyone's well-being and activities. One was to Adam Russell, whom she planned to meet at an Italian restaurant in Pimlico.

The lady he saw was considerably different from the cheerful, naughty girl he remembered from the ski slopes. Diana was undoubtedly more confident, but beneath the banter, she was a lonely and miserable young woman. 'She could really feel the cage bars chafing. At the time, she hadn't accepted them, he recalled.

Her greatest indulgence in life was sitting down with baked beans on toast and watching TV. 'That is my concept of paradise,' she informed him. Diana's new existence was marked most clearly by the presence of her Scotland Yard bodyguard at an adjacent table. It took her a long time to accept that presence; the sight of an armed police officer was the most powerful reminder of the golden prison she had now joined. She missed the little things, like the glorious moments of privacy when she could blast her favourite music on the vehicle stereo. She now had to consider another person's wishes at all times.

Initially, she would go for an evening 'burn up' in her car around Central London, leaving her armed Scotland Yard escort behind. On one occasion, she was pursued through the streets by a car full of enthusiastic young Arabs. Later, she would drive to a favourite beach on the south coast to enjoy the wind in her hair and the salty sea breeze on her cheeks. She loved being near water, whether it was the River Dee or the sea. It was where she liked to think and connect with herself.

The presence of a bodyguard was a continuous reminder of the invisible barrier that kept her from her family and friends. It was the realisation that she was suddenly a potential target for an anonymous terrorist or an unknown psychopath. The violent attempt to kidnap Princess Anne on the Mall, just yards from Buckingham Palace, and the successful break-in to the Queen's chamber by an unemployed worker, Michael Fagan, demonstrated the royal family's ongoing peril. Diana's response to this constant threat was usually straightforward. She travelled to the Special Air Services headquarters in Hereford to complete a 'terrifying' driving training where she learned the fundamental methods for dealing with a potential terrorist assault or kidnapping attempt. Her 'adversaries' threw thunderflashes and smoke bombs at her automobile to make the training as realistic as possible. On another occasion, she visited Lippits Hill in Loughton, Essex, where Metropolitan Police officers get weapons training. She learned how to use a.38 calibre Smith and Wesson revolver and a Heckler and Koch machine pistol, both of which were standard issue to members of the Royal Protection Squad.

She had learned to accept the idea of a permanent shadow; she discovered that, far from being a menace, her bodyguards were far wiser sounding boards than many of the gallant courtiers who floated around her. Sergeant Allan Peters and Inspector Graham Smith became amiable father figures, diffusing tense situations and deflating overbearing subjects with a joke or a sharp instruction. They also brought her maternal instincts to the forefront. She remembered their birthdays, wrote letters of apologies to their wives when they had to accompany her on a foreign tour, and made sure they were 'nourished and watered' when she went out with them from Kensington Palace. When Graham Smith had cancer, she invited him and his wife on a vacation to Necker in the Caribbean, as well as a Mediterranean tour on the yacht owned by Greek millionaire John Latsis.

When she was dining with friends at San Lorenzo, a favourite restaurant in Knightsbridge, one of her investigators, Inspector Ken Wharfe, would join the Princess' table at the conclusion of the dinner and entertain the crowd with his quips. Perhaps she saved her best memories for Sergeant Barry Mannakee, who became her bodyguard when she felt lost and alone in the royal realm. He noticed her confusion and became a shoulder for her to lean on, and even cry on, during this difficult time. Both Prince Charles and Mannakee's colleagues were aware of the loving bond that had developed between them. To Diana's dismay, he was transferred to other tasks just before the Duke and Duchess of York's wedding in July 1986. In the following spring, he died tragically in a motorcycle accident.

For much of Diana's unhappy early royal life, she had isolated people close to her, but Prince Charles continued to see his previous acquaintances, particularly the Parker Bowleses and the Palmer-Tomkinsons. The Prince and Princess attended the Parker Bowleses' housewarming celebration when they relocated from Bolehyde Manor to Middlewich House, 12 miles from Highgrove, and Charles frequently met Camilla when fox hunting. At Kensington Palace and Highgrove, the couple parties rarely, to the point where their butler, Allan Fisher, characterised working for the Waleses as 'boring'. It was a meagre diet: an annual dinner for Charles' polo playing friends, a 'boys only' evening, and the occasional lunch with friends such as Catherine Soames, Lady Sarah Armstrong-Jones, and Sarah Ferguson.

The tours, new houses, new baby, and Diana's ailments all had a terrible toll. In her despair, she turned to Penny Thornton, an astrologer introduced to her by Sarah Ferguson. Diana confided to Penny that she couldn't take the pressure of her position any longer and needed to quit the system. 'One day you will be permitted out, but not by divorce,' Penny assured her, confirming Diana's pre-existing belief that she would never become Queen.

In 1984, her pregnancy with Prince Harry did not ease her mood. She suffered from morning sickness again, though not as severely as the first time. Diana was still in early pregnancy when she returned from a solo engagement in Norway. She and the late Victor Chapman, the Queen's former assistant press secretary, took turns using the restroom on the journey home. He had a hangover, while she was suffering from morning sickness. During those months of waiting, she had a strong feeling that her husband was seeing Camilla again. She believed the indicators were there. Late-night phone calls, inexplicable absences, and other tiny but substantial alterations to his regular routine. Ironically, that was the happiest period of Charles and Diana's marriage. The pleasant summer months preceding Harry's birth were ones of contentment and mutual devotion. But a thunder cloud hung over the horizon. Diana knew Charles wished for their second child to be a daughter. A scan had previously revealed that her baby was a boy. It was a secret she kept until he was delivered at 4.20pm on Saturday, September 15, in the Lindo wing of

St Mary's Hospital. Charles' reply effectively ended Diana's feelings for him. 'Oh God, it's a boy,' he exclaimed, 'and he's even got red hair. With these disparaging remarks, he departed for Kensington Palace. The next day, he played polo. Diana later told friends, 'Something inside me died.' It was a reaction that signalled the beginning of the demise of their marriage.

CHAPTER 5
'I Don't Rattle Their Cages'

In June 1991, the Princess of Wales was having lunch with a friend in San Lorenzo when her bodyguard interrupted their chat. He revealed that her eldest son, Prince William, had been injured in an accident at his private boarding school. The details were hazy, but it was evident that the Prince had sustained a severe knock to the head while playing golf with a fellow student on the grounds of Ludgrove School in Berkshire. As she dashed out of the restaurant, Prince Charles drove William to the Royal Berkshire Hospital in Reading for examinations. While Prince William underwent a CT scan to diagnose the injury to his head, experts at the Royal Berkshire urged his parents to transfer him to the Great Ormond Street Hospital for Sick Children in Central London. As the convoy drove along the M4, Diana and her son rode in the ambulance, while Prince Charles followed in his Aston Martin sports vehicle. While William, who had been 'chirpy and chatty' throughout the voyage, was preparing for surgery, neurosurgeon Richard Hayward, the Queen's physician Dr Anthony Dawson, and several other doctors surrounded his parents to explain the situation. During several chats, they were informed that he had suffered a depressed fracture of the skull and needed an immediate operation under general anaesthesia. They made it apparent that there were potentially substantial risks, albeit relatively minor, both in the procedure itself and in the chance that the Prince had suffered brain damage during the initial accident. Satisfied that his son was in good hands, Prince Charles left the hospital to attend a performance of Puccini's Tosca at Covent Garden, where he hosted a group of a dozen European Union officials, including the Environmental Commissioner, who had flown in from Brussels. Meanwhile, holding his mother's hand, Prince William was brought into surgery for the 75-minute procedure. Diana waited anxiously in a nearby room till Richard Hayward entered to inform her that her son was OK. It was, she subsequently admitted, one of the longest hours of her life. As she sat with William in his private chamber, his father boarded the royal train for an overnight trip to North Yorkshire, where he was scheduled to attend an environmental study. Diana held her son's hand and watched as nurses came in every 20 minutes to check his blood pressure, reflexes, and shine a light into his eyes. As told to William's parents, the most feared adverse effect of a head injury operation is a sudden increase in blood pressure, which can be fatal. Hence the regular checkups. These were suspended about 3 a.m. when a fire alarm broke the night's calm. Diana, fatigued and agitated the next morning, was very disturbed about newspaper reports about William's possible epilepsy diagnosis. That was just one of several fears. As she discussed the subject with a friend, she observed: "You have to support your children in both good and bad times." She was not alone in her conclusion. As Prince Charles went through the Yorkshire Dales on his green mission, a phalanx of psychologists, royal monitors, and outraged moms denounced him for his actions. 'What kind of father are you?' read the headline in the Sun newspaper.

His decision to prioritise duty over family may have surprised the wider public, but not his wife. Indeed, she accepted his choice to go to the opera as normal. For her, it was just another example of a recurring trend rather than an anomaly. One friend who spoke with her minutes after William emerged from the operating room commented: 'If this had been an isolated incident, it would have been unbelievable. She was not surprised. It only verified what she already knew about him and supported her belief that he struggled to bond to the youngsters. She received no support whatsoever, no embraces, no affection, nothing.

Diana's friend James Gilbey echoed this sentiment: 'Her reaction to William's tragedy was horror and astonishment. From all accounts, it was a narrow escape. She can't comprehend her husband's behaviour, so she simply blocks it out. Diana believes: "I know where my loyalties lie: with my son."

When the Prince learned of the public's outrage, his wife was unsurprised that he blamed her once more. Charles accused her of creating 'terrible nonsense' about the seriousness of the injuries and acting innocent about the potential that the future heir to the kingdom had suffered brain damage. The Queen, who had been told by Prince Charles, was surprised and perhaps shocked when Diana informed her that, while her grandson was recovering, it had not been a straightforward procedure.

Several days after the accident, William was healthy enough to allow the Princess to visit Marlow Community Hospital as planned. As she was departing, an elderly man in the crowd fainted from an attack of angina. Diana rushed over to assist, rather than leaving it to others. When the Prince watched media coverage of Diana's sympathetic efforts, he accused her of acting like a martyr. His harsh answer exemplified the chasm between them and lent credence to Diana's observations about the media's interest in their 10-year wedding anniversary the following month. She asked matter-of-factly, 'What is there to celebrate?'

The couple's starkly contrasting public response to William's injuries confirmed what those in their immediate circle had suspected for some time: the fairytale marriage between the Prince of Wales and Lady Diana Spencer was ended in all but name. Many of their acquaintances were saddened by the demise of their marriage and the virtual collapse of their business relationships. This much-debated marriage, which began with such high promises, has now reached a stalemate of mutual blame and cold apathy. The Princess told friends that their spiritual marriage ended on the day Prince Harry was born in 1984. The couple, who had maintained separate bedrooms in their homes for years, stopped sharing sleeping quarters during an official visit to Portugal in 1987. It's no surprise that she came upon a story in Tatler magazine that asked, 'Is Prince Charles too seductive for his own good?' It's really amusing because of the inadvertent irony.

Diana considered her husband's sheer presence distressing and disturbing due to their mutual hostility at the time, according to acquaintances. In turn, he looked at his wife with apathy and hate. When a Sunday newspaper reported that the Prince had rudely ignored her during a concert at Buckingham Palace to commemorate the Queen Mother's 90th birthday, she told friends that she found their surprise weird. 'He ignores me everywhere and has for a long time. He simply dismisses me. She would never consider contributing to any of his special interests, such as architecture, the environment, or agriculture. A painful experience taught her that any ideas would be met with ill-disguised scorn. 'He makes her feel intellectually weak and inferior and regularly reinforces that message,' a close friend said. The irony of Charles taking his wife to attend Oscar Wilde's play A Woman of No Importance to celebrate his 43rd birthday was not missed on her friends. Prince Charles, a man of immense charm and humour, has an uncanny capacity to shut off people who disagree with him. That capacity was extended to a trio of private secretaries who frequently contradicted him, as well as a large number of other courtiers and personnel, including his wife. Diana's mother witnessed his ruthlessness and obstinacy at Prince Harry's christening. When he complained to her that her daughter had given birth to a boy with red hair, Mrs Shand Kydd, a woman of unwavering integrity, reminded him that he should be grateful that his second son was born healthily. Since that time, the Prince of Wales has virtually isolated his mother-in-law from his life. The event made her more empathetic to her daughter's situation. This schism between the royal couple grew too big to ignore for the sake of their public image. Before Christmas 1991, the Princess of Wales was scheduled to go to Plymouth for a rare combined public engagement. She had stayed with Prince Edward until midnight at a Mozart concert, but she cancelled the visit the next morning, claiming she had influenza. Although she felt bad after the concert, the notion of spending the day with her husband made her want to stay in bed even more.

The continual tightrope that courtiers had to tread between the royal couple's public and private lives was highlighted when the Princess of Wales was informed of her father's death on March 29, 1992, while on a skiing vacation in Lech, Austria. She was prepared to return home on her own, leaving Prince Charles to care for their children. When he insisted on returning with her, she pointed out that it was past time for him to start acting like a caring husband. In her sadness, she did not want to be part of a palace public relations campaign. For once, she dug her heels in. She sat in their hotel room, with her husband's private secretary and press secretary opposing her. They insisted that he return with her for the sake of his public image. She refused. Finally, a phone call was made to the Queen, who was residing at Windsor Castle, to settle this increasingly heated dispute. The Princess succumbed to her decision that they fly home together. At the airport, they were greeted by the assembled media, who stated that the Prince was providing his support during Diana's time of need. The reality was that as soon as the royal couple arrived at Kensington Palace, Prince Charles rushed straight to Highgrove, leaving Diana to mourn alone. Two days later, Diana drove to the burial, while Charles arrived by air. Diana's companion stated, "He only flew home with her for the sake of his public image." She believed that while she was grieving her father's death, she should be given the opportunity to behave as she wished rather than put through this farce.

According to a close friend, "She seems to dread Charles' appearance." Her happiest days are when he is in Scotland. When he visits Kensington Palace, she feels completely at a loss and like a child again. She loses all the ground she has gained when she is on her own. During those times, she had physical changes. Her speech, which was generally quick, vibrant, colourful, and forceful, degraded instantaneously when he was with her. Diana's voice became monosyllabic and flat, tinged with an indescribable fatigue. The similar tone permeated her speech when she discussed her parents' divorce and what she refers to as 'the dark decades' of her royal existence, which lasted until the late 1980s and was marked by mental trauma caused by the royal system. In his presence, she reverted to the girl she was a decade ago. She giggled at nothing, began chewing her nails (a habit she had abandoned some time ago), and assumed the hunted expression of a scared deer. The tension in their home while they were together was evident. As Oonagh Toffolo remarked, "There is a different atmosphere at Kensington Palace when he is there." The situation is stressful, as is she. She doesn't have the freedom she desires when he's there. It is so distressing to observe the stagnation there. Another frequent visitor just dubbed it 'The Mad House'.

When Prince Charles returned from a special vacation to France, she felt so oppressed that she fled Kensington Palace. Diana called a friend who was suffering the loss of a loved one. She sensed her friend was crying and responded, 'Right, I'm coming over now.' As her buddy said, 'She came immediately for me, but when she arrived, she was extremely upset. Diana informed me, "I am here for you, but I am also here for myself. My husband appeared, and I had to fly out and flee." She was in complete confusion. As far as was possible, they lived separate lives, only joining forces to preserve a facade of harmony. These reunions just afforded the public a glimpse into their solitary lives. They sat close to each other at the 1991 Soccer Cup Final at Wembley Stadium but never spoke or exchanged glances during the 90-minute game. Not long after, Prince Charles missed his wife's face and kissed her neck at the end of a polo match during their Indian tour. Even their writing paper, which previously featured a characteristic interwoven 'C' and 'D', had been replaced with individual letter headings. When she was at Kensington Palace, he would visit Highgrove or Birkhall on the Balmoral estate. At Highgrove, she had the enormous four-poster in the master bedroom, while he slept in a brass bed borrowed from his son, Prince William, because he found the extra breadth more comfortable after breaking his right arm during a polo match. Even these distant sleeping arrangements caused marital conflict. When Prince William requested his bed back, his father refused. 'Sometimes I don't know who the baby is in this family,' Diana quipped sarcastically. She no longer referred to him fondly as 'Hubcap'. As James Gilbey wrote, "Their lives are spent in total isolation." It's not like they call each other every evening and say, "Darling, what have you been doing?" It simply does not happen.

During lunch with a close friend who was also the mother of three small children, Diana described an incident that highlighted not only the status of her relationship with her husband at the time, but also her son William's protective attitude. She explained to her friend that the week Buckingham Palace decided to announce the separation of the Duke and Duchess of York was naturally difficult for her. She had lost an agreeable friend and was well aware that the media would once again focus on her marriage. However, her husband seems unconcerned about the uproar surrounding the breakup. He had spent a week touring various grand mansions to gather content for a gardening book he was writing. When he returned to Kensington Palace, he couldn't understand why his wife was so tense and melancholy. He casually dismissed the Duchess of York's departure and began into a scathing assessment of Diana's public works, particularly her visit to Mother Teresa in Rome. Even their staff, who had grown accustomed to frequent confrontations, were surprised by Diana's attitude and sympathised when she told her husband that unless he altered his attitude toward her and the job she was doing, she would have to reconsider her position. In tears, she walked upstairs to take a bath. While she regained her composure, Prince William placed a handful of paper tissues beneath the bathroom door. 'I hate seeing you sad,' he murmured.

Every day and in every way, she was plagued by her position's dilemma, divided between her sense of responsibility to the Queen and nation and her desire to find the happiness she sought. However, she believed that in order to achieve happiness, she needed to divorce; if she did, she was concerned that she would lose the children she cherished and who brought her so much joy. At the same time, she experienced rejection from the public, who were uninformed of her lonely life and took her pleasant picture at face value. It was a horribly circular argument with infinite variations and permutations, which she frequently debated with her friends and counsellors. Her acquaintances witnessed their marriage disintegrate into a conflict in which no quarter was demanded or granted. Their children and Charles' friendship with Camilla Parker Bowles were the focal points of their domestic conflicts. Officially, this feud spilled over into their public responsibilities as the Prince and Princess of Wales. She gave him nothing, and he gave less. Diana saved one statement for their most heated disagreements. 'Remember, I am the mother of your children,' she stated. That specific shell exploded during their set-piece clashes over Camilla Parker Bowles. Courtiers were frequently caught in the crossfire. When Prince Charles was nursing his wounds after the public censure of his actions when Prince William cracked his skull, his private secretary, Commander Richard Aylard, tried to make amends. In a handwritten message, he urged his royal principal to spend more time in public with his children so that he might be perceived as a responsible father. At the end of his letter, he severely emphasised in red ink and scribbled in big letters the word 'TRY'.

The plan worked for a while. Prince Charles was seen driving Prince Harry to Wetherby School and was photographed riding and cycling with his sons on the Sandringham estate. However, the Princess of Wales saw Richard Aylard's modest public relations triumph as cynical hypocrisy, given his daily participation with his children. James Gilbey explained: 'She believes he is a bad father, a selfish father, and that the children must participate in what he is doing. He will never postpone, cancel, or amend whatever he has arranged for their advantage. It's a reflection of how he was raised, and history repeats itself. That is why she is so saddened when he is spotted riding with the youngsters at Sandringham. When I told her about it, she practically had to hold back her rage since she felt the image represented the idea that he was a good father, whereas she knew the truth. She lavished William and Harry with love, cuddles, and devotion, as single parents tend to do. In her chaotic world, they provided a sense of stability and normalcy. She loved them unreservedly and completely, working with a single objective to guarantee that they did not have the same childhood that she did. The subsequent negative press led the pair to reconcile briefly in public. Prince Charles changed his schedule so that he could appear with his wife at numerous public events, including a concert at the Royal Albert Hall, and decided to spend at least part of their 10th wedding anniversary together to appease the media. It was very manufactured and barely lasted a few weeks until the truce was broken. Their complete isolation, exemplified by the appearance of the hostile 'Highgrove Set', was almost official. Charles despised her country home for more reasons than just her pals. She described her visits to their Gloucestershire house as 'a return to prison' and rarely invited family or friends. Diana's pal James Gilbey stated: "She dislikes Highgrove." She believes Camilla resides just down the street, and no matter how much effort she puts into the house, she never considers it her home. Diana took little solace in the fact that a Sunday newspaper accurately reported Camilla's whereabouts, including the unmarked Ford estate car the Prince used to drive the 12 miles to Middlewich House. Andrew Jacques, a former Highgrove police officer, confirmed this when he sold his story to a national publication. 'Mrs Parker Bowles undoubtedly looms greater in the Prince's life at Highgrove than Princess Di,' he stated, which was supported by many of Diana's acquaintances. So, who was the woman who stirred Diana's emotions? From the moment images of Camilla appeared in Prince Charles' diary on their honeymoon, the Princess of Wales harboured suspicion, bitterness, and animosity for the woman Charles loved and lost during his bachelor days. Camilla is descended from a strong county family with many aristocratic connections. She is the daughter of Major Bruce Shand, a wealthy wine trader, Master of Foxhounds, and Vice Lord Lieutenant of East Sussex. Her brother is Mark Shand, an explorer and author who used to be an escort for Bianca Jagger and model Marie Helvin before marrying Clio Goldsmith, the late supermarket millionaire's niece. Camilla is connected to Lady Elspeth Howe, wife of Lord Howe, former Chancellor of the Exchequer, and Lord Ashcombe, a rich builder. Her great-grandmother was Alice Keppel, Edward VII's long-term mistress. She was married to an Army commander and once claimed that her duty was to 'curtsy first and then rush into bed'.

Andrew Parker Bowles, who is connected to the Earls of Derby and Cadogan as well as the Duke of Marlborough, was a dashing and popular escort for society debutantes during his bachelor days. Before marrying in the Guards Chapel in July 1973, the attractive cavalry soldier was a friend to Princess Anne and Sir Winston Churchill's granddaughter, Charlotte. He was a former brigadier who had the implausible title of 'Silver Stick in Waiting to the Queen', and it was in this position that he organised the celebration procession around the Mall to commemorate the Queen Mother's 90th birthday.

Charles met Camilla in 1972 while serving in the Navy, and she was dating his polo friend, Andrew Parker Bowles, who was then a captain in the Household Cavalry. He was immediately drawn to this bright, gorgeous young woman who shared his enthusiasm for hunting and polo. According to his biographer, Penny Junor, the Prince fell completely in love with Camilla. 'She was madly in love with him and would have married him right away. Unfortunately, he never asked her. He dithered and hedged his bets, unable to resist the allure of other women, until Camilla gave up on him. It wasn't until she was gone for good that the Prince recognized what he had lost.

Camilla, now in her fifties and the mother of two grown-up children (Prince Charles is the godfather of her eldest son Tom), was seen by the public at the time as a valued royal friend. Diana constantly expressed her concerns about Camilla to her friend James Gilbey. He listened sympathetically as Diana vented her rage and despair over Camilla. He stated that she could not forget Camilla's one-time connection with Prince Charles. As a result, their marriage is a sham. Camilla's entire potential drives her to distraction. I can understand it. What on earth is that woman doing in her house? This is what she sees as the extreme injustice of the situation. Gilbey, a motor-trade executive, had known Diana since the age of 17, but they became closer after meeting at Julia Samuel's party. They talked late into the night about their different love lives, he about a failed relationship and she about her failing marriage. One of their romantic late-night phone chats from this period was ultimately made painfully public. However, in the summer of 1989, she was concerned about getting back her husband and forcing him to split up with 'the Highgrove Set'. He recalled: "There was enormous pride at stake." Her sense of rejection by her spouse and the royal establishment was clear.

At the time, she was under pressure from both her family and the royal family to make a fresh start. Diana even agreed that having another baby might help solve the problem. However, her olive branch was welcomed with the same negative apathy that had previously characterised their relationship. At times, the waves of rage, frustration, wounded pride, and rejection threatened to overwhelm her. When Prince Charles was recovering from a broken right arm in 1990, he spent his time in Highgrove or Balmoral, where Camilla Parker Bowles was a frequent guest. Diana remained in Kensington Palace, unwanted, unloved, and humiliated. She expressed her feelings to Gilbey: 'James, I'm just so tired of it. If I let it get to me, I will only irritate myself more. So the best thing I can do is become involved in my profession and get out there. If I stop to ponder, I'll go insane.

A mutual friend, who saw the royal couple's gradual estrangement, stated, 'You can't blame Diana for her fury given the fact that her husband looks to have this long-standing friendship with another lady. The marriage has fallen too far to want to win him back. It's simply too late.

Diana's improved self-confidence and revised objectives, combined with skilled counselling, helped to temper her wrath toward Camilla in the early 1990s. As her marriage deteriorated, she came to regard Camilla as a less menacing figure and more of a useful tool for keeping her husband out of her life. Nonetheless, there were occasions when she found her husband's apathy terribly hurtful. Camilla and her husband accompanied Prince Charles on a holiday in Turkey just before his polo injury, and she tolerated Camilla's regular invites to Balmoral and Sandringham with gritted teeth. When Charles came to Italy in 1991 for a sketching vacation, Diana's friends noticed Camilla was staying at another property a short drive away. When Mrs Parker Bowles returned, she made it clear that any notion of impropriety was ludicrous. During a rare family summer vacation, when the Prince and Princess and their children joined other guests on a Greek millionaire's yacht, Diana noted that her husband communicated with Camilla via telephone. They would meet socially on occasion, but there was no love lost between these two ladies trapped in an endless triangle of antagonism. At social gatherings, they made an effort to avoid each other. Diana developed a technique in public for rapidly spotting Camilla and then, depending on her mood, either watching Charles when he looked in her direction or just avoiding her gaze. 'It was a morbid game,' a pal stated. Diana knew Camilla would be attending the Salisbury Cathedral spire appeal concert days before it took place. She released her irritation in chats with acquaintances, so that on the day of the occasion, the Princess could watch her husband and Camilla's eye contact with calm delight. All those years of pent-up passion spilled out in December 1991 at a memorial service for Leonora Knatchbull, Lord and Lady Romsey's six-year-old daughter, who died of cancer. Diana was photographed in tears as she exited the service conducted at St James' Palace. She was weeping, both in sorrow and in rage. Diana was outraged that Camilla Parker Bowles, who had only known the Ramseys for a short period, was there for such a private family service. It was a point she emphasised to her husband as they returned to Kensington Palace in their chauffeured vehicle. When they arrived at Kensington Palace, the Princess was so disturbed that she skipped the staff Christmas party, which was already in full swing, and retreated to her sitting room to regain her calm. Diplomatically, Peter Westmacott, the Waleses' deputy private secretary, dispatched her friendly detective, Ken Wharfe, to reassure her. The incident at the burial ceremony highlighted her hatred of the royal system and the pretence of life at Kensington Palace. She soon aired her anger and frustration to a close friend. She stated unequivocally that her sense of duty compelled her to carry out her duties as Princess of Wales, but her tough private life caused her to seriously consider leaving the royal family. Despite the devastation of their relationship, some acquaintances believe Diana's fury and jealousy towards her husband reflected her deep desire to win him back. Those observers were the minority. Most were very pessimistic about the future. Oonagh Toffolo stated: "I had great hopes until a year ago, but now I have no hope at all." It would require a miracle. It is a great pity that these two people who have so much to offer the world cannot do so together. A friend had come to a similar conclusion after discussing Diana's problems with her for quite some time. She remarked, 'If he had done the work in the beginning and shown proper regard for his wife, they would have had a lot more going for them. However, they have reached the point of no return.

When friends discussed the Waleses' life together, they frequently used the phrase 'there is no hope'. According to one of her closest friends, 'She has surmounted all of the hurdles offered to her within the business and has perfected her public life. But the main issue is that she does not feel fulfilled as a woman because she does not have a relationship with her spouse. The ongoing tension and suspicion in their private lives inevitably influenced their public activities. The Prince and Princess were nominally a partnership, but in practice they acted individually, much like managing directors of competing corporations. As one former member of the Wales Household stated, "You very quickly learn to choose whose side you are on - his or hers." There is no intermediate ground. Courtiers can cross the magic line once or twice. Cross it too frequently, and you're out. That is hardly the foundation for a secure career.'

A similar attitude was echoed by the small army of businesspeople who passed through Kensington Palace. In 1992, David Archibald, Prince Charles' finance director, or controller, abruptly resigned. Staff at both offices believed that the main reason for his departure was the difficulty of working in an environment of mutual distrust and rivalry between the two adversarial offices. As usual, the Prince of Wales, dubbed 'Britain's worst employer,' blamed the resignation on his wife. Archibald had an excellent cause to quit. The antagonism between Charles and Diana ranged from petty to sad. The first indication of this in public came when both gave big addresses on the same day, Charles on education and Diana on Aids. One inevitably stole the thunder from the other, and such behaviour was part of a recurring pattern. When the couple returned from a combined tour to Canada in 1991, the Princess addressed several thank-you notes to the charities and government groups that had organised the trip. When they were sent to her husband to 'top and tail' with his own thoughts, he went over each letter and scratched out any reference to 'we' and replaced it with 'I' before signing them.

This was not an unusual situation. When the Prince sent a bouquet of flowers to Mother Teresa of Calcutta, who was recovering from a heart problem, in January 1992, he instructed his private secretary Richard Aylard to ensure that they were sent alone by him and not jointly. It didn't matter so much. Diana arranged a special meeting, flying to Rome's hospital to visit the woman she admired. Again, during a planning meeting for their combined journey to India in February 1992, Diana was advised to focus on family planning problems. "I think we will change your profile from Aids to family planning," said a diplomat who was impressed by her performance in Pakistan. When asked about the concept, Prince Charles complained that he wanted to lead that particular subject. Diana once urged staff to avoid 'the spoiled boy'. One of her closest friends stated, 'It's time he started seeing her as an advantage, not a threat, and accepted her as an equal partner. Her current position within the organisation is quite lonely. Consultation between the pair was always confrontational, taking place in an atmosphere of reciprocal blame. It was so unusual to have a calm talk about difficulties that when the Prince approached Diana to read a private report made by a senior courtier regarding staff abuses of the royal name, the Princess, who was accustomed to cold indifference, was taken aback. There was fear that the royal name and notepaper were being exploited to obtain clothing discounts, theatre tickets, and other benefits. While the situation necessitated sensitive handling, the most unexpected aspect of the episode was the relationship between the Prince and Princess. While their regular business relationships were characterised by intrigue and competitive hostility, Diana felt a sense of obligation to her husband. When he returned to public life in 1991, after a lengthy recovery from a broken arm, he planned to issue a bizarre statement about the considerable speculation around his injury. He told his team to find a fake arm with a hook on the end so he could appear in public as a real-life Captain Hook. Senior courtiers advised Diana, concerned that Charles might make a fool of himself. She advised obtaining a false arm, but he conveniently misplaced it shortly before attending a medical appointment in Harley Street, Central London. While Charles was irritated by the deception, his staff was happy that his dignity had been maintained due to Diana's prompt intervention. It would be a mistake to think that the Prince and Princess of Wales battled on equal terms. The Princess may have been more appealing to the press and the public, but inside the palace walls, she was reliant on revenue from her husband's Duchy of Cornwall to fund her private office, and her junior status within the royal hierarchy meant that Prince Charles always had the final say. The Prince of Wales eventually decided on everything, including her attendance at his planning meetings, the makeup of joint overseas tours, and the office structure. When she suggested forming a 'Princess of Wales Trust' to raise funds for her several charities, William rejected, knowing that it would detract attention and money from his own Prince's Trust charity.

During the Gulf War, the Princess and her sister-in-law, the Princess Royal, independently devised the plan to visit British troops stationed in the Saudi Arabian theatre of operations. They intended to fly out together and were looking forward to going over the desert in tanks and meeting the boys in khaki. However, Sir Robert Fellowes, the Queen's private secretary, interfered. The plan was scrapped because it was deemed more appropriate if a more senior royal represented the family. So Prince Charles flew to the Gulf, while the Princess of Wales was tasked with travelling to Germany to meet the spouses and families of troops.

The continual needle and edge in their working relationship was matched by the veil of secrecy that the duelling offices draped over their competitive operations. Diana had to use all of her guile to extract information from her husband's office before flying to Pakistan for her first major solo foreign tour in 1991. She was scheduled to make a visit in Oman, where Prince Charles was attempting to entice the Sultan into sponsoring an architecture college. Diana was naturally curious and eager to learn more, but she recognized that approaching Prince Charles or his senior aides directly would result in a dusty answer. Instead, she sent a brief message to the Prince's private secretary, Commander Richard Aylard, asking whether she required any briefing notes for the short layover in Oman. As a result, when she was on official Foreign Office business, the Prince was forced to exhibit his hand.

In this atmosphere of sullen distrust, concealment was a necessary and persistent companion. Caution was her watchword. There were plenty of eyes, ears, and police video cameras to capture the sound of an angry voice or the appearance of an unexpected guest. Tongues wag, and stories spread with electrifying efficiency. This is why, while learning about her bulimic condition, she concealed publications on the issue from curious eyes. She dared not bring home tapes from her astrology readings or read the satirical magazine Private Eye, which had a cruelly realistic description of her husband, in case it drew negative attention. The phone was her lifeline, and she spent hours chatting with friends: 'Sorry about the noise, I was trying to get my tiara on,' she told one concerned friend.

She was a hostage to fortune, held captive by her public image, constrained by the constitutional condition of her unique position as Princess of Wales, and imprisoned by her daily life. Her friends defined the abbreviation POW as 'prisoner of war'. Indeed, the oppressive claustrophobia of royal life only exacerbated her natural dislike of tight quarters. This was made clear to her in 1991, when she went to the National Hospital for a body scan because her doctors suspected she had a cervical rib, a benign growth that frequently traps nerves beneath the shoulder blade. Like many patients, she became quite nervous once inside the enclosed scanning equipment and needed to be calmed down with a tranquilliser. It meant that a 15-minute surgery took two hours. She started sending scented candles instead of thank-you notes to those who provided products and services in case her well-meaning words ended up in the wrong hands. Again, before going skiing in Austria with her children and friends Catherine Soames and David Linley in 1992, she was hesitant to invite Major David Waterhouse. She had consoled him during his mother's burial in January and hoped that a vacation would help him cope with his grief over her passing. Diana, who had been observed in his company on a frequent basis, was concerned that his presence would be misinterpreted, putting his own life under unnecessary scrutiny. So she didn't invite him. Although her children brought her great joy, she was also aware that they were her passport to the outside world. She could take kids to the theatre, the movie, and the park without drawing negative attention from the media. There were some negatives, though. When she took Prince Harry and a group of pals to see Jason Donovan in the musical Joseph and the Amazing Technicolor Dreamcoat, the Princess had to wait outside the gentlemen's restroom during the intermission for her charges. She had to approach her social life with caution. While her husband had been able to go about his private life unnoticed for years, Diana was acutely aware and unhappy that every time she was seen with an unattached male, no matter how innocently, it became headline news, such as when she spent the weekend at Philip Dunne's parents' country estate. There was no relief. She had to cancel a lunch engagement with her friend Terence Stamp after learning that his flat in Albany was being staked out by press photographers. Diana's internal foes were the courtiers who observed and critiqued her every move. If Diana were the present star of the Windsor roadshow, senior courtiers would be the producers, hovering in the background, ready to condemn her every slip. When she visited her mother in Italy for three days, Antonio Pezzo, a handsome member of the family who hosted her, drove her around. As she said her goodbyes, she impulsively kissed his cheek. She was chastised for the gesture, much as she was for applauding Prime Minister John Major's behaviour during the Gulf Crisis. It was a human reaction to his difficult position as a new Prime Minister, but Sir Robert Fellowes, the Queen's private secretary, thought it was sufficiently political to warrant negative commentary.

The tiniest infraction of royal protocol was cause for complaint. Following a film premiere, the Princess visited a party and had a lengthy talk with Liza Minnelli. The following morning, she was reminded that attending these events was not customary. However, the celebration did have one positive outcome. She appreciated her interaction with the Hollywood diva, who spoke at length about her terrible life and simply stated that anytime she felt low, she thought about Diana and it helped her persevere. It was a heartfelt and honest chat between two ladies who had been through a lot in their lives, and it served as the foundation for their long-distance friendship.

It was no surprise that the Princess, who was naturally trustworthy, placed little trust in the royal structure. When she returned from her morning swim at Buckingham Palace, she opened much of her personal correspondence in order to learn firsthand what the general public was thinking. She no longer had to rely on her staff's cautious filter. This policy yielded some satisfactory results. A message from a father whose kid was dying of Aids really moved her. The young man's dying wish was to meet the Princess of Wales. His father wrote to Diana in June 1991, but had little expectation of success. After hearing his plea, Diana personally arranged for his son to join an Aids hostel in London managed by the Lighthouse Trust, which she was about to visit. Her considerate deed fulfilled his last wish. If the letter had been processed normally, the family would have likely received a compassionate but noncommittal response from a lady-in-waiting.

She gradually phased out these conventional royal helpmates, whose duties included accompanying her on public engagements and performing administrative tasks, because of her lack of confidence in them. She began using her elder sister Sarah in this capacity - she joined the Princess on an important visit to Budapest, Hungary, in March 1992 - or going on what she called her 'Away-days' on her own. One friend commented, "She had these terrific run-ins with her ladies-in-waiting, particularly Anne Beckwith-Smith (her one-time private secretary)." She felt that they were holding her back by being overly protective and "in" with the system.

Instead, she chose to consult those who were peripheral to the system. She would occasionally call Major-General Sir Christopher Airey at his Devon residence for guidance. Airey, who was unexpectedly fired as Prince Charles' private secretary in 1991, was well-versed in the system's workings and could lead her wisely. For a period, Jimmy Savile boosted her public image, while Terence Stamp provided general speech writing advice. She also depended on a group of unofficial counsellors, who chose to remain unknown, to brainstorm ideas and problems. They polished her speeches, advised on sensitive staff issues, and provided fair warning of potential publicity troubles.

She was drawn to outsiders exactly because she felt disconnected from the royal system. According to James Gilbey, "She gets along much better with them than the men in grey because they [the men in grey] are tied up in preserving a system that she believes is outdated." There's a natural confrontation there. They are attempting to maintain something, and she is attempting to flee.' Her astrologer Felix Lyle observed: 'She has a flying spirit and optimism that is readily defeated. Dominated by individuals with strong character, she lacks the self-confidence to challenge the system.

Another friend agreed, stating, "The entire royal business terrified her." They gave her no confidence or support.' As her confidence grew, she realised that she couldn't reach her full potential under the existing royal constraints. She told friends, "Inside the system, I was treated very differently, as if I were an oddball." I thought I wasn't good enough. Now, thank God, I believe it is acceptable to be different.

Diana lived a perplexing double existence, praised by the public but watched in uncertain and frequently envious silence by her husband and the rest of his family. The world thought she had cleaned up the dowdy image of the House of Windsor, but within the royal family, which was raised on ideals of control, distance, and formality, she was regarded as an outsider and a liability. She was tactile, emotional, slightly irreverent, and spontaneous. For a white-gloved, stiff-upper-lip institution with a giant 'Do not touch' sign hanging from its crown, the Princess of Wales posed a threat. Her past experiences had taught her not to trust or confide in members of the royal family. She learned that blood bonds are most important. As a result, she maintained a deliberate distance from her in-laws, skirting issues, avoiding confrontations, and confining herself in her ivory tower. It was a double-edged blade since she failed to bridge any gaps, which is critical in a closed culture tainted by family and office politics. She had few allies among the royal family. 'I don't rattle their cages and they don't rattle mine,' she explained.

So, despite her affection for Scotland and her upbringing in Norfolk, she found the environment in Balmoral and Sandringham completely draining of her energy and vitality. Her bulimia was at its worst during these family vacations, and she would try everything to get away for a few days. Diana experienced the truth that lies beneath the monarchy's apparent image of unwavering togetherness. She knew that in secret, the current Court was not much different from earlier reigns, with its squabbles, feuds, and infighting.

The Queen Mother and her daughters, the Queen and Princess Margaret, form a close-knit and unwavering trio at the core of the royal family. As author Douglas Keay pointed out in his profile of the Queen, 'Cross one and you cross them all.' Diana's relationships with these three important figures were strained. She had a lot of time for Princess Margaret, a neighbour at Kensington Palace who she acknowledged as being the most helpful in adjusting to the rarefied royal society. 'I've always adored Margo,' she explained. "I love her to bits, and she's been wonderful to me from the beginning."

Her relationship with the Queen Mother was far less friendly. Diana viewed her London residence, Clarence House, as the source of all negative comments about herself and her mother. She maintained a wary distance from this matriarchal figure, portraying social gatherings held by the Queen Mother as stiff and excessively formal. Diana's grandmother, Ruth, Lady Fermoy, the Queen Mother's lady-in-waiting, testified in court about her daughter's inability to care for her four children. The judge accepted her perspective on Frances Shand Kydd, and antagonism and bitterness within the Spencer family persisted for a long time. At the same time, the Queen Mother, who had a negative attitude toward Diana and her mother, wielded immense power over the Prince of Wales. Diana was effectively excluded from the mutual admiration society. 'The Queen Mother drives a wedge between Diana and the others,' according to a friend. 'As a result, she uses any reason to avoid her.'

Diana's relationship with the Queen was far more amicable. However, it was influenced by the fact that she was married to her eldest son and future ruler. Diana was first afraid of her mother-in-law. She adhered to the conventional obsequies, offering a deep curtsy every time they met, but otherwise maintained her distance. During their few and tense discussions about the Waleses' troubled marriage, the Queen suggested that Diana's recurring bulimia was a cause, not a symptom, of their problems.

The Sovereign also hinted that the instability in their marriage was the most important factor in any thoughts she had regarding abdication. Naturally, this irritated Prince Charles, who refused to talk with his mother for several days after she stated in her 1991 Christmas broadcast that she intended to serve the nation and the Commonwealth for some years to come'. For a man who reveres his mother, silence was a measure of his rage. Once again, he blamed the Princess of Wales. As he marched around Sandringham's corridors, the Prince complained to anybody who would listen about the status of his marriage. Diana pointed out to him that he had already abdicated his legal responsibilities by appointing his brothers, Princes Andrew and Edward, as counsellors of state, the officials stand-ins' for the Sovereign when she is away on official business. If the Prince was so unconcerned about these nominal constitutional duties, she questioned softly, why should his mother give him the job?

In the early 1990s, the Queen and her daughter-in-law developed a more casual and amicable relationship. At a garden party in 1991, the Princess felt confident enough to crack a joke about the Queen's black hat. She congratulated her on her choice, mentioning how it would be beneficial during funerals. In a more serious tone, they had intimate chats about her eldest son's mental health. At times, the Queen found his life's direction unfocused, and his behaviour strange and chaotic. It did not escape her notice that he was as dissatisfied with his situation as his wife.

While Diana saw the monarchy as a failing institution at the time, she admired the Queen's conduct during her reign. Indeed, as much as she wanted to leave her husband, Diana told the Queen, 'I would never let you down.' Before attending a garden party on a hot July afternoon in 1991, a friend handed Diana a fan to bring with her. She refused, stating, 'I can't do it. My mother-in-law will be standing there with her handbag, gloves, stockings, and shoes.' It was a remark stated in admiring tones for the Sovereign's complete control in every situation, no matter how difficult.

At the same time, the Princess had to deal with various crosscurrents within the family. Diana had a friendly relationship with Prince Philip, whom she considered a loner, but she knew that her husband was scared by his father. She acknowledged that his connection with his eldest son was 'problematic, very tricky'. Charles wished to be patted on the back by his father, whilst Prince Philip would have preferred that his son consult him more frequently and at least acknowledge his contribution to public discourse. It irritated Prince Philip, for example, that he initiated the public discussion about the environment, but Prince Charles gained the audience.

Diana, like her father-in-law, maintained a distant but polite connection with her royal sister-in-law, the Princess Royal. Diana understood firsthand the challenges that a royal woman faced within the organisation and had nothing but appreciation for her independence and efforts, particularly on behalf of Save the Children Fund, of which she is president. While their children frequently played together, Diana would never have thought to confide in the Princess or call her for lunch. She was happy to see her during family gatherings, but that was the extent of their relationship. The media made a fuss at Prince Harry's christening because Diana's decision not to designate Anne as a godparent was interpreted as an indication of their strained relationship. The Princess was not approached because she was already the boys' aunt, and her status as godparent would simply repeat matters. The two Princesses, like the rest of the royal family, were constantly divided. Diana is an outsider by birth and inclination, whereas Anne was born within the system. From time to time, the Princess Royal demonstrated where her ultimate loyalty lay. In 1991, a conflict at Balmoral highlighted the two commoners' isolation: the Princess of Wales and the Duchess of York.

That altercation, which occurred on a bright August evening while the family was enjoying a barbecue on the grounds of Balmoral

Castle, brought to light the developing tensions and conflicts within their ranks. There was anxiety over an incident in which Diana and Fergie raced each other around private roads in the Queen Mother's Daimler and a four-wheel drive estate car. The argument got considerably more personal, with a primary focus on the Duchess of York. She bolted. Diana said on Fergie's behalf that marrying into the royal family was extremely tough, and the Duchess found it harder the longer she stayed within their boundaries. She urged the Queen to grant the Duchess more flexibility, underlining that she was at her wits' end. Fergie confirmed this shortly afterwards, telling friends that 1991 would be her last visit to Balmoral. She was true to her word. Eight months later, the Duke and Duchess announced their separation.

It was a stark contrast to the Duchess of York's first visit to the Queen's summer retreat five years previously, when she had wowed the royal family with her passion and vigour. Diana had watched, often compassionately, as her sister-in-law was pummelling by the media and overwhelmed by the royal system, which had progressively drained her energy. At times, the Duchess of York's erratic behaviour resembled comedy rather than life mimicking art. As her clothes, mothering instincts, and ill-chosen companions came under fire, the Duchess sought assistance from a variety of clairvoyants, tarot card readers, astrologers, and other soothsayers to navigate the royal maze. She was introduced to several by her friend, Steve Wyatt, the adopted son of a Texas oil magnate, but she discovered many on her own. Her frequent visits to Madame Vasso, a spiritualist who heals sick minds and bodies by seated them under a blue plastic pyramid, exemplified the influences on this more restless and unhappy person. Some days, she had her fortune told and her astrological transits analysed every few hours. She tried to conduct her life according to their forecasts, her turbulent spirit clinging to any semblance of solace in their thoughts. While Diana, like many members of the royal family, was captivated by the 'New Age' approach to life, she did not follow every prophecy. The Duchess, on the other hand, was completely enthralled by their results and eagerly discussed them with her companions. As a result, Diana played Othello, while the Duchess played Iago. She was an incessant voice in Diana's ear, whispering, beseeching, and imploring, predicting tragedy and doom for the royal family and asking her to flee the royal institution. It was not an exaggeration to say that the Duchess of York spent almost every week analysing the newest developments with her sister-in-law, close friends, and advisers. When the Prince and Princess of Wales' marriage came under increased investigation in May 1991, Fergie's Spooks', as her friends call them, predicted that Prince Andrew would soon become King and she would become Queen. While the Duke was enthused about the idea, his wife grew disillusioned with her role. The claustrophobia of the royal realm was too much for a woman who was used to catching planes like other people hail cabs. In August, her soothsayers predicted a difficulty with a royal car, and in September, an impending royal birth would cause a crisis. Specific dates were specified, but even when they passed without event, the Duchess remained confident in her oracles. By November, there was talk of a death in the family, and as Diana prepared to spend Christmas at Sandringham with the royals, the Duchess told her that she and Prince Charles would have a disagreement. He would attempt to walk away, but the Queen would stop him. Interspersed with these ominous forebodings was an almost daily drip, drip, drip of pleading, reason, and wish-fulfilment as the Duchess begged the Princess to join her and quit the royal family. Her invitation must have been appealing to a lady in an untenable situation, but Diana had learnt to trust her own judgement. In March 1992, the Duchess chose to formally split from her husband and depart the royal family. The Princess was saddened and alarmed by her friend's acrimonious marriage collapse. She witnessed firsthand how swiftly the Queen's courtiers might turn against her. They brutally assailed the Duchess, accusing her of behaving inappropriately for the royal family and citing several situations in which she attempted to profit from her royal connections. Courtiers even erroneously claimed that the Duchess had engaged a public relations firm to promote her departure from the royal family. As a BBC correspondent put it, 'The knives are out for the Duchess at Buckingham Palace.' It was a foreshadowing of what Diana would face if she followed in her footsteps.

CHAPTER 6
'My Acting Career Is Over'

For many years, there was little laughter and even fewer smiles at the Kensington Palace apartments where the Prince and Princess of Wales lived in London. Visitors were quick to notice the bleak atmosphere, and terms like 'dead energy', 'gloomy', and 'tense' became prevalent in their descriptions. Diana told pals, "I feel like I've died in that house many, many times." Even her bedroom exuded misery. 'I can imagine her lying in bed at night clutching her teddy and crying,' one former staff member said of one small girl's bedroom, which was littered with gazing toy animals from a similarly sad past.

She was now separated not just from her husband, but also from much of the anguish that her marriage had caused her. Perhaps symbolically, her first decision was to get rid of the mahogany double bed she had slept in at Kensington Palace since her wedding 11 years ago. Then she painted the bedroom, installed new locks, and changed her personal phone number. Her new life alone had begun.

During the winter of 1992, there was a lot of back-and-forth between Highgrove, Kensington Palace, and St James's Palace as the couple's personal belongings were returned to them in their now bachelor houses. One Palace official described it as "an undignified and very sad finale to the fairytale." The Prince and Princess, who had received an Aladdin's Cave of presents before their marriage, unceremoniously burned undesired belongings. A bonfire of their vanities was lit in the grounds of Highgrove, and valuable objects were transferred to Windsor Castle or donated to charity. Only a few mementos from Prince Charles' time at Kensington Palace remain.

Prince Charles' wife was not even allowed that tiny memorial. Over the next six months, every indication that she had ever resided at Highgrove was meticulously removed. A designer was subsequently commissioned to totally redesign the mansion, as well as the Prince's new residence at St James's Palace. Visitors who visited Highgrove couldn't help but note that there were no pictures of the Prince of Wales' estranged wife among the hundreds of family photos.

In the months following the separation, frequent visitors to Kensington Palace began to observe a shift in the formerly desolate Apartments Eight and Nine. The staff looked nicer, less formal, and the environment was lighter and more casual. There were also minor decorative changes: walls were repainted, terracotta pots with moss and twig arrangements appeared, and Prince Charles' austere military and architectural paintings were replaced with delicate landscape and dancing paintings. Guests were greeted with loud music and the aroma of freesias or white Casablanca lilies. The dominant mood was unavoidably more feminine, though Diana never really resolved to follow her first desire and entirely renovate her home.

The Princess had a love-hate connection with her residence at Kensington Palace, just as prisoners do with their captors. The Palace represented so much accumulated pain and heartache to her, but, as she told friends, 'I feel secure here.' Throughout her marriage, she described her first-floor sitting area as my hideaway, empire, and nest'. In reality, it was a shrine to the two men in her life: Princes William and Harry. A five-foot leather rhino cushion sat in front of the fireplace for them to lie on while watching television, while images in wooden or silver frames depicting the lads go-karting, in tanks, on horseback, cycling, fishing, on police bikes, or in school uniform adorned every available surface. More framed portraits, this time of her late father, Earl Spencer, her sisters Jane and Sarah, and her brother Charles, the current Earl, graced the mantelpiece. There were also pictures of the Princess herself in this gallery, including a signed black-and-white photograph of her dancing with film director Richard Attenborough, another with singer Elton John, a third with Liza Minnelli, and privately taken photos of her impersonating Audrey Hepburn in Breakfast at Tiffany's outfits.

The room was crowded with cosy groups of pottery animals, enamel boxes, and porcelain figures, giving the sense that it belonged to a woman attempting to protect herself from the intrusions of the outside world. A girlfriend described the room as "like an old lady's room, packed to the gunwales with knick-knacks." You can barely move. Another close friend highlighted the attitude behind this profusion: 'It's quite normal for people who come from shattered homes to desire material stuff around them. They're creating their own nests. Diana's warm, somewhat self-deprecating sense of humour helped to relieve the overall atmosphere of claustrophobia. Every chair had silk cushions embroidered with humorous motifs such as 'Good girls go to heaven, bad girls go everywhere,' 'You have to kiss a lot of frogs before you find a prince,' and 'I feel sorry for people who don't drink because when they wake up in the morning, that is the best they will feel all day.' Her toilet and lavatory were covered with newspaper cartoons depicting Prince Charles talking to his plants and their visit to the Pope in the Vatican; they, too, provide insight into what she thought hilarious.

However, even these modest touches could not mask her overall discontent, which was reflected in her ambiguous attitude toward her home. For months after the breakup, she vacillated between wanting to stay at Kensington Palace and wanting to live on her own in the country. The idea of living in an open jail at Kensington Palace, continuously monitored by servants and police, gnawed at her spirit. She yearned to be free, but she was also aware of the perception that the press and the general public would have of her purchasing her own home; it would appear to be such a stark departure from everything that had occurred since her marriage began in 1981. According to a friend, one of her main concerns is a strong fear of disapproval and condemnation. So, as always, she drew back.

By the spring of 1993, Diana was growing increasingly dissatisfied with her situation at Kensington Palace. So she was 'happy and delighted' when, in April, her brother Charles, Earl Spencer, offered her the Garden House, a four-bedroomed mansion on the Althorp estate. It was an offer that also neatly avoided the issue of her being perceived to be excessive. 'At long last, I can construct a comfortable nest of my own,' she told friends, ecstatic about the prospect of furnishing and decorating her own home; indeed, the urge to make the property 'cosy' became her continuous mantra. For the first time, she would be able to express herself without having to look over her shoulder or be reminded of painful memories. She approached a family friend, Dudley Poplak, a South African-born designer who had designed the interiors of the Kensington Palace apartments she shared with Prince Charles. They explored colour schemes, fabrics, and wallpapers; soft blues and yellows were tentatively picked. The exhilarating prospect of a new life unfolded before her. Furthermore, the Garden House had additional benefits. It was not overlooked by any other structures on the estate, giving her complete privacy, and, best of all, the ubiquitous armed bodyguard would not have to encroach on her new home because there was a tiny house nearby where he could be stationed. Diana's beautiful new world came crashing down just three weeks later. Earl Spencer called her and said he was no longer comfortable with the proposal. He contended that the increased police presence, cameras, and other surveillance would result in unacceptable levels of intrusion. With Althorp accessible to the public, her freedom of movement would be subject to a variety of constraints. Diana was surprised and at a loss for words. While her brother's arguments were absolutely reasonable, for her, his decision meant far more than just losing a property. Her 'cosy nest' had signified both a challenge and a fresh start; more than that, the Garden House had literally been the house of her dreams. For several months, the Princess and her brother had a cold relationship. Relationships in the Spencer clan had never been easy. Her parents' divorce, followed by her father's remarriage to Raine, Countess of Dartford, daughter of the romance author Barbara Cartland, left the family unhappy and divided. Diana had never forgiven her grandmother, Ruth, Lady Fermoy, one of the Queen Mother's ladies-in-waiting, for testifying against her own daughter - and Diana's mother - Frances during the painful divorce proceedings. When Prince Charles and his granddaughter split, Lady Fermoy once again failed to support her own flesh and blood. The family was astounded to learn about Diana's two visits to Lady Fermoy's Eaton Square apartment in June 1993, barely three weeks before the latter died. Rather than allowing her hatred to boil, the Princess chose to address the woman who had so horribly harmed her. They were naturally unpleasant and frigid conversations, with Lady Fermoy noticeably taken aback by Diana's brave choice to tackle the concerns that had driven them apart, rather than engaging in frivolous light talk while the underlying difficulties remained unspoken. It would be an exaggeration to claim that these discussions resulted in a reconciliation, but they did result in a truce between the two warring factions. Diana's willingness to develop bridges reflected her determination to lay to rest the demons of her past. This newfound commitment was at the heart of her reconciliation with her stepmother in May 1993. Diana, her sisters, and brother felt little affection for the woman they referred to as 'Acid Raine'. When her father died, the Princess might have easily dismissed her stepmother, but she chose not to do so, instead inviting Raine and her new husband, Count Jean-François de Chambrun, to lunch. It was an emotional encounter that represented a watershed moment in their relationship, yet their subsequent frequent meetings were met with hostility by the rest of the Spencers, culminating in an intense confrontation with her mother, Frances Shand Kydd. During this exchange, Diana pointed out that if she could hate Raine the most and still forgive and forget, the rest of the family should be able to too. Diana's success in removing some of the emotional brushwood from the past freed her to begin setting the groundwork for a new existence. Her dream had been built around a new home, and its failure caused her a devastating blow. Her aspirations dashed, the Princess spent several months licking her wounds, enduring but not enjoying life at Kensington Palace, which by now had an ambiance that one royal employee dubbed 'Bleak House'. She had become, in a sense, a prisoner of her own creation, a slave of her mind. She had gained some freedom, if not full liberty. The door of the golden cage was open. She now needed to find the motivation to start anew. Instead, she appeared to be half-living the old. It was, in reality, a peaceful, almost monastic existence. The Princess' daily routine remained relatively consistent. Her day began promptly at 7 a.m. After a light breakfast of pink grapefruit, homemade muesli or granary toast, or fresh fruit and yoghurt with coffee, she left for her daily workout at the prestigious Chelsea Harbour Club. She never showered at the club, preferring to change at home, away from prying eyes and any camera lenses. Around 9 a.m., her colourful hair stylist, Sam McKnight, appeared. He was one of the few guys in her life who could keep the Princess waiting while yet making her smile. While he worked on her hair (a change in style always meant a change in the path of her life), the Princess was on her bedroom phone, because pals knew that early morning was the best time to catch her. At that time of day, she was usually sociable and upbeat. By the evening, however, when the events of the day had worn her down and depleted her emotional batteries, making conversation might be, as one friend put it, 'like pushing glue uphill'.

Every day, she had to cope with a deluge of correspondence with the assistance of her private secretary, Patrick Jephson, and her secretaries. Diana insisted on opening much of the mail herself. There were letters from both her charity and members of the public. These, usually in a reserved tone, included homilies, felicitations, and tales of tough personal experiences. Many of them really moved the Princess, who would frequently respond personally. In any case, she was a diligent correspondent, remembering dozens of birthdays each year and, as her friend Rosa Monckton put it, 'sent thank-you letters more swiftly than anyone else I know'. Jephson recalled: 'After a trip, she may write to your wife and apologise for taking him away. She could be both an inspiring and demanding boss, and she frequently demonstrated remarkable generosity to those she worked for. She enjoyed calling pals starting around 10 a.m. Lord Palumbo, her lawyer Lord Mishcon, the Duchess of York, and, after their reunion, her stepmother Raine were frequent callers. If she was feeling down, bored, or lonely, she would go shopping to brighten herself up. There were also monthly visits to her therapist, Susie Orbach, at her North London home, as well as what the Princess referred to as 'Pamper Diana' days, during which she indulged in various New Age therapies. She might go out to eat for lunch with pals or have a business lunch at home on occasion. Most of the time, she ate a simple supper alone at Kensington Palace. After lunch, she may receive formal visitors from her charities or the regiments she was affiliated with, or she would spend an hour or so catching up on correspondence, leaving her butlers to handle the frequent phone calls. She would occasionally visit her offices at St James' Palace or drive to the boys' schools to watch them play on their sports teams. On summer afternoons, she would sit in the garden for hours, enthralled in the latest best-selling novel. Diana knew in her Kensington Palace fastness that every time she left the safety of her own door, she became a captive to fortune. She occasionally went to the movies with a few pals, but she postponed a trip to What's Love Got To Do With It?, a film about Tina Turner's abusive relationship with her husband, for fear that her choice of film would be misinterpreted. She frequently spent her evenings alone, retiring to bed to have a small supper from a tray while watching television.

Her friends were concerned about her increasingly lonely life. 'Such loneliness, she doesn't know who she can trust,' said her friend Lucia Flecha de Lima, wife of Brazil's former ambassador to the United Kingdom. The Princess's global prominence further exacerbated her sense of emotional isolation. 'She feels imprisoned, not just in a goldfish bowl, but in her own reality, a cage with no way out and no shoulder to weep on. A counsel stated, "It is a terrible place to be."

She missed her children a lot, especially during customary family celebrations. On Christmas Day 1993, a little more than a year after the separation was announced, the Princess spent Christmas Eve with the boys in Sandringham, the Queen's Norfolk hideaway, but bravely left for Kensington Palace on Christmas morning. Back in London, she had her Christmas lunch alone before going for a dip at

Buckingham Palace. The following day, she flew to Washington to spend a week with Lucia Flecha de Lima. Diana recounted, 'I sobbed all the way out and all the way back, I felt so horrible for myself.'

Her weekends were, if anything, quieter than her weekdays, except when the lads visited. According to the rules of the separation, the Princess would see the boys on alternating weekends when school holidays allowed. Diana would collect them up from Ludgrove, then Eton, and drive them back to London for nursery tea. Like other kids, they sat transfixed to the latest action movies on satellite television, which the Princess had installed so they wouldn't miss their favourites. After dinner, the lads watched a rented movie, such as Rambo (Arnold Schwarzenegger was a hero), or played the computer game Nintendo before retiring to bed.

William and Harry ate breakfast with their nanny every Saturday and Sunday had roughly 8.30 a.m. Even when the young Princes were there, the Princess maintained her own schedule, with the nanny in charge of dressing. When they were ready, they could join their mother at her gym to learn to play tennis, or they could stay at home and ride their BMX bikes on the Kensington Palace grounds, or they could let off steam in vigorous water-pistol fights, spraying each other with hosepipes, or having pitched water-bomb battles with schoolmates. There were other distractions, too, especially when their mother's schedule permitted her to take them on outings. Harry's main pastime at the time was go-karting on a Berkshire circuit. As a sportsman, he was fearless, eager to run William down. The older prince preferred to go riding or shooting with his pals, where he would not be continuously disappointed by his failure to outperform his younger brother. He is, in any event, the more serious of the two, whereas Harry is more agile and mischievous in both sports and conversation. Despite the fact that Harry cruelly ridiculed his older brother, he urgently needed him.

When the boys were with their father or had returned to school, Kensington Palace's apartments resumed their usual stillness. The only thing that broke the cloistered atmosphere was the harsh sound of the telephone, which served as the Princess' confessional, best friend, and occasional doom. Diana was deeply embarrassed and distressed by the publication of the Squidgy tape. Now it was Prince Charles' turn to regret the creation of the telephone. The Prince's public image had suffered significantly in the months leading up to the separation, and in January 1993, tabloid newspapers published transcripts of a tape-recorded telephone conversation allegedly between the Prince and Camilla Parker Bowles on December 18, 1989. Its intimate and repulsive nature prompted many senior Establishment individuals who had previously been loyal to the Crown, including members of the Church, the military, and Parliament, to question Prince Charles' competence to rule.

The late-night call demonstrated the couple's unwavering love for one another, not least through its occasionally childishly vulgar intimacy. Following the woman's several endearments, the man says: 'Your great achievement is to love me,' adding, 'You suffer all these indignities, tortures, and calumnies.' The woman responds, 'I'd go through anything for you. That is love. It is the strength of love. The man makes a crude joke about being transformed into a tampon so that he can be constantly connected with his sweetheart, Camilla Parker Bowles, the wife of one of his oldest friends. Just before he hangs up, he says he will 'push the tit', which refers to one of the phone's buttons. The woman says, 'I wish you were pressing mine.' He replies, 'I love you, I adore you,' and the woman responds, 'I do love you.' Significantly, neither the Prince of Wales nor Mrs Parker Bowles have ever denied that the tape was authentic.

For some time, Prince Charles' acquaintances tried to explain the whispered phone calls, clandestine meetings, and covert gifts between Charles and Camilla as acts of friendship. Diana, on the other hand, had always relied on her intuition and observations. She was also aware of a cache of love letters written on Camilla's headed writing paper, evidence that could not be easily refuted. Despite her certainty that the taped discussion was authentic, she was surprised to see the dirty details put out in black and white. She read the transcript with increasing rage, recognizing the names of so many individuals she had known and trusted for years, who had collaborated to deceive her by providing cover stories or safe locations where the Prince and Camilla could meet in secret.

The recording fed the Princess's ongoing fascination with the connection that had put such a pall over her marriage. She claimed to be unconcerned about Prince Charles and Camilla Parker Bowles' fate, but she was keeping a close eye on them. With her astrologer, she studied Camilla's chart - she, like Diana, is a Cancer - with a sick and obsessive obsession with the couple's fate.

The Princess put up a brave face in public, but in private she was a grieving lady, lamenting her lost innocence, a broken relationship, and the wasted years of her adult life. Diana believed she could defy the royal system and make better use of her position during periods of optimism. At other times, she would burst into tears, inspired by a sentimental film or an innocent comment that reminded her of all the agony of the past. It was also evident that she began to wear dark colours, particularly black, which was unusual for someone who placed such a high value on colour. Isolated and lonely in her cocoon at Kensington Palace, she succumbed to drift and indecision.

The breakdown of her marriage, her awareness of the hostility directed at her by many in royal circles, particularly Prince Charles', her obsession with her husband's affair, and her often meaningless life within the depressing atmosphere of her home all contributed to a deep loneliness and a destructive lowering of her self-esteem. Another aspect contributing to the Princess' profound and growing isolation was her continued struggle to find a fulfilling public role. In March 1993, she flew to Nepal for five days on her first official abroad tour since their separation. The media focused on the evidence that she was being treated as a second-class royal, failing to see that the low-key, informal aspect of the visit was what Diana had specifically chosen.

The Princess unwittingly created a persona for herself that would eventually become a phenomenon. Almost alone among major members of the royal family, she grasped the public's yearning for a more modest and relevant monarchy, which matched with her goals of remaking her royal public life to her own liking. Overseas employment she found exciting, not only because it provided her with a different stage than that of her husband, but also because it removed her from the glare of Buckingham Palace. During the early days of her separation, both the Princess and the Palace were unsure about her future plans. Nobody could take away her constitutional position as the future king's mother. However, her public function was uncertain. 'People's agendas changed overnight,' she remarked. I was suddenly the Prince of Wales' separated wife, a problem and a burden. "How will we deal with her? This has not happened before."'

Whatever the Queen's soldiers felt about Diana, their primary responsibility was to serve the Sovereign and her son while maintaining the status quo. To that aim, they, like the Prince of

Wales's associates, attempted the onerous work of restoring his public image at the expense of lowering the standing of the Princess, whom they readily conceded was still the shining light in a waning royal constellation. If their idea for the Prince's job conflicts with his estranged wife's vague objectives, then be it. Diana began to notice that travels overseas were being prohibited and letters were suddenly going missing. When she expressed a desire to visit British troops and refugees in Bosnia under the auspices of the Red Cross, she was told that Prince Charles' plans to go there came first. Then, in September 1993, she was told that she couldn't go to Dublin to meet the Irish President, Mary Robinson, for security reasons', but two months later she went to the Remembrance Day service in Enniskillen, Northern Ireland, which could be an infinitely more dangerous trip.

Diana suspected that the Establishment did not want her to have such a strong public image, as this would surely eclipse her estranged husband. Furthermore, she was certain that 'the enemy' was conducting a campaign against her. 'The enemy was my husband's department, because I always got more publicity,' she claimed. However, the Princess was no royal rebel. She had learnt enough during her decade at the Firm to follow the party line. She was aware that the men in grey' at the Palace viewed her popularity as a threat to the Prince of Wales, but she wanted to do good. I was never planning to harm anyone. I was never going to disappoint anyone.'

It was a stressful position, aggravated by her dissatisfaction with a system that discreetly stifled or marginalised her initiatives and goals. Her annoyance reached a climax that autumn after a series of supportive media pieces on the changing face of the monarchy, which were based on briefings to journalists by Sir Robert Fellowes and other palace officials. In one article, an anonymous courtier was cited as saying patronisingly: 'Diana is obstinate, but we must show her love and sympathy and bend over sideways to avoid a chasm in the early stages because, if she became bitter and twisted, it would be impossible for the children.' Furious with her portrayal as a dumb child, she reacted furiously to her brother-in-law, Fellowes, telling him that she was sick of being used by the Palace as press fodder, and that this type of narrative simply fueled conjecture about her life. In any case, during 1993, the war of the Waleses was fought both in the media and behind the scenes, with Prince and Princess striving to win the hearts and minds of the nation. By the summer, nine officials were working directly or indirectly on Prince Charles' portfolio of well-publicised interests or to improve his image. In contrast, the Princess, whose staff was funded by the Prince's estate, the Duchy of Cornwall, had only a part-time press officer. Nonetheless, she was accused of being a media junkie, rushing from one picture call to the next: a Caribbean vacation, a long flume ride at Thorpe Park Leisure Centre, or skiing with her children. For a princess accustomed to an adoring media, this shift in fortune harmed her already fragile self-esteem and exacerbated her anxiety. Her overconfidence in her astrologer's predictions demonstrates how little she valued her own senses and judgement.

Diana had an awful summer. She began the year with a surge of vigour, but as the months passed, the relentless criticism, both inside and beyond the Palace, wore her down, as evidenced by her lacklustre attitude to everyday royal chores. The never-ending series of handshakes, tree-planting, small conversation, and smaller children seemed both boring and futile to her. At the end of June, the Princess decided to cease her 'Awaydays', or visits outside of London. A photo call during a July visit to Zimbabwe, in which she was pictured handing out food to youngsters, exemplified her great unhappiness with the ridiculous circus. She believed that the activity patronised the children and reinforced the 'begging-bowl' image of Africa. She pledged it would not happen again.

Diana spent a lengthy summer holiday, first in Bali and later with her boys in America, contemplating her future. She arrived home, invigorated, to find hostile headlines and frightening news from the palace. Prince Charles had recruited a surrogate mother to take her place while the youngsters were staying with him.

Diana was furious. Already on the fringes of royal life, she was now being undermined in her most gratifying function. She watched in quiet as Alexandra 'Tiggy' Legge-Bourke planned outings for the boys, took them shopping, and entertained them. She winced when she saw media photos of Harry sitting on Tiggy's knee and trembled at the thought of Tiggy calling the boys my babies'. Tiggy posed an even greater threat because she was Diana's age and social rank, and she got along well with Prince Charles' pals.

The long-standing anger was brought to a head more than three years later at a Christmas party, when Diana made a statement to the boys' nanny about her relationship with Prince Charles. Tiggy was in tears and later issued a solicitor's letter to the Princess, demanding an apology for the 'false charges'. It was a horrible experience. Tiggy appeared to reflect everything Diana despised about the royal establishment and its attempts to take her children away. Fortunately, before her death, Diana came to accept Tiggy's active role in her boys' life. At the moment, however, she believed the wolves were circling for the kill. Her opponents had degraded her rank, personality, and position. They now wanted the one thing she valued most in her life: parenthood.

Diana began planning her departure from public life in the autumn. The Princess was at her wits' end, confused by the animosity of the media that had once praised her, battered by the Palace machine, and continually looking over her shoulder at Prince Charles' camp. Her emotional anguish spilled over into public outrage. 'You make my life terrible,' she said to a photographer as he took photos of her and her children leaving a West End cinema. She pushed his chest and jabbed her finger into his face before returning to William and Harry. The event was one of several heated exchanges with professional cameramen.

However, an amateur photographer proved to be the final straw. If she had been hesitant to retire from the public eye previously, she was convinced when she saw a full-page picture of herself working out at her former health club on the front page of the Sunday Mirror in early November. She had long suspected that these images existed, but it was nevertheless shocking to see herself, clothed in a leotard, being exploited in this manner. The images were discreetly taken by the gym's manager, Bryce Taylor, a New Zealand businessman. Their publication was a flagrant infringement of privacy, but Taylor was compensated a six-figure sum. Buckingham Palace, MPs, several newspaper editors, and Lord McGregor, Chairman of the Press Complaints Commission, all expressed their outrage at the guilty newspaper group. The princess felt betrayed and violated. "Bryce Taylor pushed me into the decision to go," she explained. 'The images were simply horrifying.'

She was enraged when Taylor had the audacity to pretend that she had secretly wanted the photographs taken. The Establishment's antipathy toward her was so strong that numerous influential columnists and politicians began to suggest that Taylor's charges that the Princess was manipulating the press had some merit. Neither did the fact that she had taken the unusual step of asking her attorneys to sue Taylor and Mirror Group Newspapers deter her opponents. It was another sign to her that no matter how hard she tried or how innocent her deeds were, a disease of cynicism was slowly ruining the public's opinion of her. All of this strengthened her resolve to break free from the fickle and gloating media that had long held her in their grip. Months later, her stand was justified, and the newspaper donated a considerable sum to charity.

On Friday, December 3, 1993, during a charity luncheon benefiting the Headway National Head Injuries Association, the Princess announced her retirement from public life. After more than a decade in the spotlight, she asked for 'time and space' in a quavering but uncompromising voice. During her five-minute address, she made a special point on the constant media attention: "When I began my public life 12 years ago, I realised that the media might be interested in what I did." I recognized then that their attention would inevitably turn to both our private and public lives. But I had no idea how overwhelming that attention would become, or how it would affect both my public and personal lives in such a difficult way.

As she later stated, "The pressure was intolerable at the time, and my job, my work, was being affected." I wanted to devote 110 percent to my task, but I could only provide 50. I owed it to the public to say, "Thank you; I'm going to disappear for a while, but I'll be back."

Indicating that she would continue to support a small number of charities while she worked to rebuild her private life, the Princess emphasised: 'My first priority will continue to be our children, William and Harry, who deserve as much love, care, and attention as I am able to give, as well as an appreciation of the tradition into which they were born.'

Diana never mentioned her estranged husband while thanking the Queen and the Duke of Edinburgh for their 'kindness and support'. In private, she was clear about who was to blame for her exit from the stage. 'My husband's family has made my life terrible for the past year,' she informed a pal.

Diana arrived at Kensington Palace that afternoon feeling relieved, heartbroken, and quietly elated. Her retirement would allow her much-needed time to ponder and concentrate. If the separation had given her hope for a new life, her departure from royal duties would allow her to turn that optimism into a dynamic new career, one that would fully utilise her undeniable abilities of compassion and caring on a larger, international scale. A few months later, during a reception at the Serpentine Gallery, where she was a patron, the Princess was in good form. She was at ease, humorous, and cheerful in the company of her friends. The events of 1993 seemed like a distant memory. As she spoke with movie actor Jeremy Irons, he told her, 'I've taken a year off acting.'

Diana grinned and responded, 'So have I.'

CHAPTER 7
'Tell Me Yes'

It began by chance, as have so many important events in Diana's life. A casual conversation with her divorce solicitor Maggie Rae led to a covert meeting with the then-opposition leader, Tony Blair, and, finally, the resolution of the subject that had dominated her thoughts for months: her desire to become a humanitarian ambassador.

It was an aspiration that had been burning within her for a long time before she openly expressed it during her only television appearance in 1995. Her long-standing devotion to finding a place as a princess for the world rather than the Princess of Wales revealed much about her sense of national responsibility while also graphically displaying her evolution as a woman and, perhaps shockingly, as a feminist. During her early years in public life, she was content to meet society's - and the monarchy's - expectations for a princess. Essentially, royal males are judged by what they say, and royal women by their appearance. Diana's appearance, more than her accomplishments, identified her as a natural beauty as she matured. For a long time, she accepted the role of subservient helpmate to her husband. She was commended for just being. For being, not doing. One of her friends noted, "She was only expected by the royal system to be a clothes horse and an obedient wife."

The breakup in December 1992 altered everything. Unlike Prince Charles, whose constitutional position as the future King is well defined, the Princess had no predetermined duty or lodestar to guide her. Semi-detached from the monarchy, she was flying solo for the first time in her adult life, fully aware that it would be a difficult journey. 'I will make mistakes,' she stated, 'but that will not prevent me from doing what I believe is right.'

It was a process that included both letting go of her regal background and acknowledging her own strengths and limitations. One of Diana's many perplexing contradictions was that, while she did not value herself highly as an individual, she understood her worth on the public stage, recognizing that her standing in society, both at home and abroad, provided her with a unique platform to support the causes and issues she cared about. However, she was thoroughly dissatisfied with the etiquette, flummery, and farce that always surrounded monarchy. Her challenge was to reinvent her public character, to remove the robes of her position while maintaining her authority. According to a close acquaintance, 'She felt she was being held back by the system and unable to reach her actual potential.'

Essentially, the source of her anger was the British monarchy's manner and style, the brittle formality and mind-numbing irrelevance of so much royal life. The Princess instinctively believed that if she could modify the tone of her public life, she could improve the substance of her commitment to the country. 'I want to help the man on the street,' she once stated, reflecting the reality that she was a woman who was happier with the people than with her own. 'I feel far closer to people at the bottom than to people at the top, and they [the royal family] don't forgive me for it,' she stated soon before her death. Her competence in public life was the intuitive ability to utilise her position to advance her interests, while her natural inclination drew her to the dying, diseased, and dispossessed. It was a formidable combo. 'I will never complain again,' she declared as she emerged from a one-room, airless cabin in a Himalayan village in Nepal on her first solo abroad tour in 1993. She aspired to a more informal, relaxed, and approachable royal manner; 'This needs a woman's touch,' she declared, revealing a growing feminism in both her private and public life. In essence, she believed that so many conflicts and problems in a male-dominated world sprang from the aggressive, secretive, and often insensitive masculine ego. She believed that incorporating female attributes such as intuition, compassion, compromise, and harmony into the equation would help to address problems more successfully. Her thinking, influenced by New Age advisers, was also rooted in her jaded view of the monarchy as a male-dominated institution, her undoubted cynicism toward the opposite sex following the failure of her marriage, and frequent private visits to the Chiswick refuge for battered women. Her passion in women's concerns was matched by a growing realisation that she had a unique role to play on the global stage. It was amazing and exhilarating. Her efforts for Aids and leprosy showed that she could overcome national lines, and her bravery in disclosing her eating disorders inspired many suffering around the world to seek help. Many people thanked her for assisting them in dealing with their own problems, which she found both uncomfortable and rewarding. Against this growing worldview, the

Princess shared her views for a future role with then-Prime Minister John Major and Foreign Secretary Douglas Hurd. She desired a travelling ambassadorial role with a humanitarian rather than political focus. Diana believed that blocked conversations between conflicting parties were the root cause of so many confrontations. Her solution was that the female touch may pour oil on turbulent waters and assist clear congested routes of communication. Simplistic, perhaps grandiose, but the idea of the Princess functioning as a humanitarian ambassador received a positive response from the Prime Minister, who forwarded the suggestion to Buckingham Palace for consideration. They respectfully notified Downing Street that this was an ideal post for the Prince of Wales. "We want the heir, not her," said the men in grey'.

It's no surprise that Diana recognized a parallel to her own situation in Nigel Short's match against Boris Kasparov at the World Chess Championship. I adored the game; it is my life. "I'm just a pawn pushed around by the powers that be," she remarked. Even though she thought her objectives were stifled by the British Establishment, her work was not overlooked overseas. At a ceremony in New York in December 1996, Dr. Henry Kissinger awarded her with the 'Humanitarian of the Year' award, complimenting her strength and 'luminous personality' for having 'associated herself with the ailing, the suffering, and the disadvantaged'.

Diana, like others before her, regarded herself as a prophet without honour in her own land. This irritation had previously bubbled out in her famous Panorama television appearance, in which she appealed to the public over the heads of the Palace. She stated plaintively, 'I'd like to be an ambassador for our country. With all of this media attention, let us not sit in this country and be beaten by it. Let's take these folks to represent our country and its positive traits overseas. I've been in a privileged position for 15 years. I have a lot of knowledge about people and how to communicate, and I want to apply it. While her views may have gone unheard within the government and Palace, others were listening. As divorce proceedings progressed following the Queen's intervention in December 1995, Diana unavoidably spent a lot of time with her solicitors, developing a strong bond with Maggie Rae, her legal adviser who was leading her through the complexities of the case. By coincidence, Maggie, Cherie Blair's former flatmate, is a close friend of the Blairs and, encouraged by Diana, agreed to serve as an informal channel between the Princess and the Opposition leader. Tony Blair, who was watching her blossom from the wings, saw Diana's exceptional ability to represent Britain on the global stage. 'She was the face of the youthful New Britain he intended to construct,' says a Blair adviser. However, tremendous caution had to be exercised when scheduling face-to-face meetings because any leak would have been extremely damaging for both Tony Blair and Diana. Several encounters were scheduled, with Blair more struck by her humanitarian instincts and international appeal. When Blair became Prime Minister in May 1997, he had the opportunity to officially utilise Diana's evident talents by hosting a weekend summit at Chequers, the Prime Minister's official country retreat, in the summer. While Prince William played football with the Blair sons on the lawn, the Princess and the Prime Minister discussed the specifics of her informal ambassadorial position. Diana was overjoyed, remarking later, 'I hope I will finally have someone who knows how to use me. He has told me he wants me to go on various missions. I really want to go to China. I am really skilled at sorting people's heads out. What impressed the young Prime Minister the most was her amazing ability to get to the heart of a complex subject without raising too many political hackles. As he stated after her death: 'She had a wonderful ability, as we saw with the land-mine situation, to walk into a potentially contentious area and immediately clear for everyone what was the correct thing to do. That was an exceptional attribute in and of itself, and I believed there were numerous ways it could have been harnessed and used for the benefit of others. More than anything else in the last few weeks of her life, the Prime Minister's enthusiastic support and encouragement of her work, as well as the success of her campaign against the evils of landmines, gave her a revitalised feeling of self-worth and a more defined path in her public life. Her employees were the first to notice the change in mood. 'Her passion was persistent and contagious,' said her secretary, Louise Reid-Carr. Her engagement in the landmine crisis, like her agreement with Blair, was a matter of timing. By happy coincidence, Diana's friend, film director Lord Attenborough, invited her to a charity premiere of his film In Love and War, a moving documentary about the devastation caused by landmines on civilians, particularly women and children, at the same time that the Director-

General of the British Red Cross, Mike Whitlam, was visiting Kensington Palace to secure a renewed commitment to the organisation. Diana was captivated by the film, which concentrated on the Red Cross's work, and she quickly volunteered to assist raise funds for the mission to rid the world of landmines. Furthermore, she opted to accompany Red Cross officials and a BBC video crew to showcase the charity's work in war-torn Angola. Diana would have described it as a very grown-up project. Before flying to Africa, the Princess voiced fear that her activities could be perceived as political. Lord Attenborough recalled: "She was aware of the potential political pitfalls, but decided to take the risk on the grounds that the suffering caused by landmines should be brought to the public's attention." Diana inevitably raised political hackles by championing the fight to ban landmines - one junior minister in the then-Conservative government described her as a 'loose cannon', and Tory MPs' objections prevented her from attending a meeting of the all-party landmine eradication group in the House of Commons. Typically, the Princess kept curiously distant from her accusers. 'I am a humanitarian. I always have been, and I always will be," she stated simply. Furthermore, by contributing her weight to the effort, she was definitely making a difference. Pictures of her going across a minefield in Angola sparked global attention; 'The impact she made was absolutely fantastic,' according to the British Red Cross. Enthused by this initial success, the new British government responded by prohibiting the export and use of landmines, while the Clinton administration was pressured into a similar policy shift. The Princess discussed visits to other countries, including Cambodia, Thailand, Afghanistan, northern Iraq, and Bosnia. Finally, following advice from the Foreign Office, she chose to pay a three-day visit to Bosnia, which was still recovering from the civil war, with the acclaimed journalist Lord Deedes. He remembers not only her soft sense of humour, but also her ability to listen and express the incomprehensible. When she walked through Sarajevo's largest cemetery, she came upon a mother maintaining her son's grave. He wrote, 'There was no language barrier'. The two women softly embraced. Watching this sight from a distance, I wondered who else could have done it. Nobody.'

However, the 40-odd cameramen and journalists who trailed around the ruins of a once-proud nation were less concerned with the sober issues surrounding landmines than with the explosion of interest in Diana's new man, Dodi Fayed, the playboy son of Mohamed al-Fayed, the controversial owner of Harrods department store. It was a poignant reminder to Diana, if she needed one, that while she may have fled the royal family's smothering embrace and reinvented her public character, she would never be free of her enduring and encompassing image as a beautiful, unmarried, and accessible young lady. Whether she liked it or not, who she was going to marry had a greater intrigue than what she was about to say. Furthermore, since her separation in December 1992, the Princess has had to learn to live with a society that is uncomfortable with strong, assertive women. More than one critic noticed that Charles and Diana's breakup triggered a "backlash of misogynistic indignation that was truly shocking." She knew that if she was discovered in a thoughtless caress or innocent embrace with another man, the whispering campaign would start. This was not an exaggeration, as seen by the quasi-ritual humiliation suffered by the separated Duchess of York when photos of her having her toes sucked by her financial adviser John Bryan were publicised.

Diana's main anxiety, until the divorce was finalised and the details of settlement were clarified, was that her children would be snatched away from her by Britain's most powerful and feared family. So she was forced to practise extreme prudence, such as never holding dinner parties at Kensington Palace because they would be misinterpreted, with any unattached males present being fair game for an ever-vigilant media. Indeed, whenever she wished to see a male visitor at Kensington Palace, she would usually insist that they go in the boot of her car to evade the photographers. As she constantly grumbled, "Who would take me on?" I have a lot of baggage. Anyone who invites me to super must accept that their business will be reported in the newspapers. I suppose I'm safer alone.

She was acutely and frequently angrily aware that her tracks were being followed by paparazzi photographers looking for the jackpot first photo of the Princess with the new man in her life. Her caution was warranted. Regardless of how innocent her associations were, she knew from painful experience that male buddies suffered for a long time, if not forever, as a result of media attention. She'd almost lost count of how many guys - and often their spouses - had made front-page news after spending a casual evening with her at a cinema, theatre, or restaurant.

Her emotional disposition made an already problematic situation worse. The Princess was a touchy, affectionate, and needy woman who longed for the warmth and companionship that a meaningful relationship might provide but had been denied for far too long. For most of her adult life, she was confined to a frigid and distant marriage, forcing her to channel her feelings elsewhere, purchasing generous gifts for friends and surrounding herself with worldly belongings to ease her solitude. So, like many single mothers, she was overly protective of her sons, overly familiar with her staff because she was lonely, and unnervingly open with complete strangers in her charitable work. As a friend remarked, "She is always doing everything for everybody else; she needs to start doing things for herself." She seeks praise and adultery for being a martyr due to her deep insecurities.

Her façade of sophisticated glamour and unapproachable sexuality concealed her deepest need for a man to adore, care, and love her. Unwanted as a newborn and hated as a bride, she only wanted a man she could rely on, a companion she could trust. Diana, on the other hand, had only experienced a romantic existence of betrayal and disloyalty, whether by fate or design. When she had trusted, she had been disappointed, and when she had loved, she had been brutally exposed. She was spurned by Prince Charles for another lady; her former bodyguard Barry Mannakee, on whom she relied, was tragically assassinated; James Gilbey's friendship was cruelly and publicly exposed in the Squidgygate tapes; and her lover, Captain James Hewitt, sold his story. Her friendship with former England rugby captain Will Carling ended when his wife Julia, a TV personality, blamed her for their marriage's breakdown, and her relationship with art dealer Oliver Hoare ended abruptly following a police investigation into a series of nuisance phone calls to his home. Only her ties with Dr Hasnat Khan, a heart surgeon, and property developer Christopher Whalley appeared to be unharmed. Her reluctance to dive headfirst into a full-fledged love affair was understandable.

Despite the pain and betrayal, the Princess, who was at heart a guileless, naive young woman, maintained a romantic picture of her future, dreaming of a knight in shining armour who would sweep her away to a new life. 'Her intellect tells her she wants to be the world's ambassador, but her heart tells her she wants to be wooed by an adoring billionaire,' a pal wisely observed. At the same time, she was acutely aware of the upheaval that a new union would cause, both within the royal family and among her two sons. She once told her husband, 'If I fall in love with someone else, the sparks will fly, and God help us.' Her primary concern was for her sons. Any potential suitor for her hand needed to get their approval before he could genuinely capture her heart. One of James Hewitt's enticing qualities was his ability to get along with William and Harry. While she desired two more children, ideally girls - she was thrilled when her astrologer predicted that she would have another child in 1995 - her desires were balanced by her concern for the impact on her existing family.

Thus, her constant dream of finding a mate to share her life was balanced by caution stemming from her experience, position, and existing family. 'I haven't taken this long to get out of one bad marriage and into another,' she told gossip journalist Taki Theodoracopulos. This tightness in her emotions revealed itself in her numerous sessions with astrologers, where she sought a sign, a feeling of her future. She was always asking them to anticipate the type of man she would one day marry. 'Whoever you are, come here,' she would reply lightheartedly. While many prophecies were completely wrong, the essential predictions, those she sincerely believed, now have an unsettling, cockeyed accuracy. A common element in these prophecies was that she would marry a foreigner, or at least a guy of foreign descent. France occurred several times in her private astrological forecasts, both as a future home and as the birthplace of the new guy in her life. Indeed, one of the reasons she pondered relocating to France, South Africa, or America was not just the unwanted media attention at home, but also the promise of new love, happiness, and optimism away from her native shores, as predicted by her astrologers.

Her ruminations about the future were balanced by her reflections on the past. She spent hours with her friends debating whether Charles and Camilla would ever be happy together, or whether he would ever have the guts to give up the kingdom for the woman he loved. Her obsessive curiosity was balanced with sympathy for their suffering. 'He will not give her up, and I wish him the best,' she once told a friend. "I'd like to say that to his face someday." As time passed, she came to terms with Camilla's role as châtelaine at Highgrove and realised that the Prince's public acceptance of their relationship should reward her dedication and prudence. However, as she mourned a lost youth and innocence, her attitude shifted quickly to censure or self-pity. So when the Prince announced that he would be hosting Camilla's 50th birthday party at Highgrove in July 1997, Diana decided to stay away. While she put on a brave face for the event - 'Wouldn't it be amusing if I suddenly appeared out of the birthday cake?' she joked - she knew that the media attention would simply rehash old scars and rekindle old hurts.

In this mood, she accepted Mohamed al-Fayed, the owner of Harrods department store,'s standing invitation for her and the boys to join him, his wife Heini, and their four children at his holiday property in St. Tropez, South France. Even though Fayed, a notorious character whose contributions to select Members of Parliament helped bring down the Conservative government, had known the Spencers for years, several of her friends, including Rosa Monckton, wife of the Sunday Telegraph's editor, persuaded her not to accept. The Egyptian multi-millionaire, who has been denied British citizenship despite frequent protests about the unfairness of the exclusion, employed Diana's stepmother, the Countess de Chambrun, in his store and had grown so close to Diana's father, the late Earl, that he would boast that they were like brothers. While he is harsh and dictatorial in business, as those who have dealt with him would tell, Diana only saw the warm, generous, and affectionate side of his personality. She was delighted to be pictured with his arm around her while they stood on the deck of one of his yachts in St. Tropez. Diana appeared relaxed and carefree, completely oblivious to the cameras as she jet-skied or swam off the beach in front of Fayed's villa.

However, media criticism that the Princess had selected a questionable and improper holiday host stung her. She approached a boatload of British journalists and said that they had been harsh to Fayed, a long-time family friend, as well as unfair to her and the boys, and asked if they might leave them alone. In a last statement, she warned, 'Expect a great surprise in the coming two weeks.'

It was an occurrence that appeared to capture both her unworldly innocence and her continual fragility. She was stupid to anticipate privacy in the company of a man who was a thorn in the flesh of the

British Establishment, in the most fashionable resort in southern France, during the height of summer. At the same time, she was constantly on the lookout for a safe haven, especially during school breaks, where she and her boys could spend time together before the Princes returned to their father at Balmoral. Perhaps if she had purchased her own country property - for a period, she looked for properties in Berkshire near William's public school, Eton - or realised her ambition of living on the Althorp estate, she would have approached holiday invites from well-meaning friends with caution.

Four days into that tragic July trip, Fayed's eldest son, Emad, also known as Dodi, joined the party. Dodi had first met the Princess 10 years ago when he played polo with Prince Charles. When he was introduced to Diana, there was little evidence of their subsequent familiarity. Crew members saw that he bowed and addressed her as 'Ma'am', showing her the respect she deserved for her position. Indeed, Dodi had his own yacht anchored alongside Jonikal, his father's boat, where he was sleeping with his then-girlfriend, Californian model Kelly Fisher.

At first glance, the 41-year-old playboy, a Hollywood film producer, seemed an improbable suitor for the hand of a princess, a woman who had spent her life removing the phoney gloss of royalty in order to spend time with and actually understand individuals on the fringes of existence. Dodi, the only son of Mohamed al-Fayed and his first wife, the late Samira Khashoggi, whose brother Adnan is a rich arms dealer, was given his own Rolls-Royce complete with chauffeur and bodyguard when he was only 15 years old. After attending premium schools in Switzerland, France, and Egypt, he completed his training at the Sandhurst Royal Military Academy to 'toughen him up' before joining the United Arab Emirates Air Force.

As a young man with a taste for fast automobiles and attractive women, it was unavoidable that he would be drawn to the gleaming glamour of Hollywood, where he became a film producer, most famously on the Oscar-winning Chariots of Fire. Following the breakdown of his eight-month marriage to model Suzanne Gregard, he was linked to a string of glamorous women, including Brooke Shields, Joanne Whalley, Cathy Lee Crosby, and Julia Roberts. Kelly Fisher, his holiday companion, was the most recent in a long string of love affairs. Though he once said that his first marriage had put him off the institution forever, it appeared that he was ready to settle down with the Californian model. She later stated that he had really considered marrying her and purchasing a Malibu home together. He even purchased her a $200,000 ring and gave her a $200,000 check, which bounced, as proof of his long-term plans.

Outwardly, Dodi Fayed was the quintessential frivolous playboy, skimming across the surface of life, buying fame and friendship as he purchased his five Ferraris with his father's rumoured $100,000 per month allowance. Diana, on the other hand, was able to delve under the surface of his personality and uncover characteristics that may have reminded her of her first love, Prince Charles.

Aside from their mutual passion for polo, both men shared other remarkable similarities, such as growing up in the shadow of strong, controlling dads. This led to them both participating in dangerous activities as a way to prove themselves and please their fathers. While Dodi was readily dismissed as an idle gadfly, at least until he met Diana, Prince Charles' life was one of drift and indecision, with rambling utterances and unfocused thoughts. His anguish over the murder of his 'honorary grandfather', Lord Mountbatten, also impacted his life. Diana's first impression of the future king was that he was a sorrowful man, which surely won her over. Those who knew Dodi well say that beneath the gentlemanly charm and courtesy that Diana appreciated in Prince Charles, there was a man with a sorrowful soul. His sensitivity was linked to the tragedies he had faced in his life, specifically the deaths of his mother, whom he cherished, and several other close relatives. Diana was drawn to this combination of anguish and sensitivity, and she reacted intuitively when she saw other people's pain.

Dodi's relationship with the boys was equally vital to their personal chemistry. He booked a disco for two nights so Diana and her children could dance in privacy, and others who saw him with William and Harry at La Renaissance café in St. Tropez observed that they seemed at ease in his presence. Later, they all travelled to an amusement park and played bumper cars.

By now, the formality and distance that had defined their first few days together had given way to a pleasant closeness, with the couple speaking amicably and easily together. 'They were calm, full of knowing looks, and obviously comfortable together,' remarked one crew member. Before heading to Milan to join Elton John and other celebrities at Gianni Versace's funeral, Diana said simply and directly, 'It was the happiest holiday of my life.'

As their connection grew stronger, Mohamed al-Fayed openly expressed his desire for his eldest son to be with the world's most renowned woman. 'I did give them my blessing,' he admitted, as the possibility of a link between his family dynasty and the upper levels of British society became ever closer.

Meanwhile, Prince Charles' shadow hung in the backdrop. In an odd manner, his decision to 'come out' in public with Camilla by holding her 50th birthday party appeared to give Diana licence to be open about her own love life as well. Diana's animosity toward Camilla was fading, and the friendly equilibrium she had reached with Prince Charles, combined with the new direction and success of her public life, all pointed to the same conclusion: Diana was not only finding inner peace, but also preparing for the man she so eagerly awaited to enter her life. In short, she was prepared for romance.

The rapid outbreak of this love affair caught everyone off guard, much like a rainstorm on a calm summer day. "Don't worry, I'm not going to elope," she told a friend as she took off in a Harrods jet for a cruise off the Sardinian coast alone with the new man in her life. For the first time since her divorce, Diana no longer felt the need to conceal her love affair, and she welcomed the news that the photographers had captured long-range photos of the couple hugging and kissing. She told friends that in Dodi, who was so warm, caring, and attentive, she had finally met a man who valued her for herself and cared only about her happiness.

Even Kelly Fisher's tearfully broadcast allegations that Dodi had dumped her for Diana, which should have raised red flags, had little effect on her feelings. There were soon more concerning stories from America, and different previous girlfriends spoke openly about his eccentricities, one even claiming that he had threatened her with a gun, but Diana remained unconcerned. All the time, shadowy figures assisted the media by offering remarks purported to 'friends' emphasising the couple's growing intimacy.

When she flew to Bosnia on her landmines campaign, again using a Harrods plane, the couple spoke via satellite cell phones. 'She smiled and laughed with him,' recalled Sandra Mott, who hosted the Princess on her three-day visit. As Dodi told his ex-wife Suzanne Gregard, "Diana and I are having a romance, a real romance." A shift in his personality emphasised these sentiments. Dodi's longtime acquaintances saw that he appeared more settled and serious, ready to make his relationship with Diana succeed. 'I'll never have another girlfriend,' he told Fayed's spokesman Michael Cole, who then publicised the discussion.

What began as a silly-season narrative was now treated more seriously, as seen by the couple's flight in Dodi's helicopter to see her psychic, Rita Rogers, a close adviser to Diana and the Duchess of York. Her closest friends were perplexed that she was sharing so sensitive details about her life with a man she had only known for a short period. While Dodi flew to Los Angeles to settle the Kelly Fisher fiasco, she discreetly sailed to the Greek islands with her friend Rosa Monckton on a Harrods aircraft. Despite the fact that she had not made any decisions about her future, her friend could see Diana was pleased for the first time in years, enjoying herself with a man who clearly and publicly cared about her. Nonetheless, she was deeply dissatisfied with the manner in which he showered her with gifts. 'That is not what I want, Rosa; it makes me uneasy. I don't want to be purchased; I already have everything I desire. I simply want someone to be there for me, to make me feel safe and comfortable. It undoubtedly brought up sad memories of her childhood, when she desired nothing materially but everything emotionally, as well as her relationship with her late father. Her father showered her with gifts, but she felt he was not there when she needed him. On one occasion, she recalled a conversation he had in 1991 while flying to Paris to buy a birthday present for her. 'I don't want that; I only want you,' she said to him. Whatever discomfort Dodi's expensive lifestyle caused her, the Princess, who is famously generous with her friends, purchased her partner a cigar cutter from Aspreys, the London jewellers, etched with the words: 'With love from Diana'. As a further expression of her affection, she gave him a pair of cufflinks that belonged to her father. The day before her funeral, a Fayed spokeswoman stated, "She said that she knew that it would give him joy to know they were in such safe and special hands."

As whirlwind relationships go, this one was a cyclone. The pair had only been together for a week, but the media was already discussing marriage, fueled once again by careful leaks from unknown sources. It was far from one-sided, with Diana's inherent caution and disdain of showy consumption overshadowed by Dodi's apparent affection, care, and sensitivity. With him, she no longer felt lonely. Elsa, I adore him. I've never been happier,' the Princess informed her companion, Lady Elsa Bowker. She even contacted her answering machine from her cell phone just to hear his 'beautiful voice'. On August 21, the pair sailed to the Mediterranean and boarded Fayed's boat, the Jonikal, for their second trip alone that month. Once again, certain journalists received information about their anticipated arrival and departure timings, while photographers captured Diana and Dodi walking across the beach in St. Tropez.

The intimacy and tenderness of their body language as they lazed around on a jet-ski in the bay, Diana slinging her leg over Dodi's shoulder, demonstrated the closeness of their connection. More significantly, they were able to avoid the paparazzi and go window shopping in Monaco. Diana was particularly fascinated by a diamond ring in the display of Alberto Repossi's jewellery store on Place Beaumarchais. The ring, a huge diamond surrounded by a cluster of smaller stones and priced at £130,000, was part of the 'Tell Me Yes' collection of engagement rings. Diana was supposed to have said, "That's the one I want." It was unclear whether the ring represented a longer-term union, or a hint that she had finally achieved true peace and contentment. While she may have been comfortable, peace remained elusive. As the pair drifted off Portofino, the infamous paparazzi snapped them carousing on the deck of the 195-foot Jonikal. Their intrusions raised alarms, but images of the Princess sunbathing on the yacht's diving platform were widely circulated throughout the world. 'only tell me, is it bliss?' Rosa Monckton asked Diana on her cell phone on August 27th, only days before she died. Her reply said it all: "Yes, bliss." Bye-bye.' She seemed to have everything. Humanitarian success on the global scale, contentment, and love in her own life. As she lazed on the deck of the Jonikal, the barometer of her heart was calibrated correctly. By some strange alchemy, the people recognized this shift, that this lonely, vulnerable, and rudderless vessel had last found a soothing anchor in life, a safe harbour to escape the hazards of the sea.

For a few brief days, she relished that condition of grace in a turbulent existence. Then the heavens opened, claiming her.

CHAPTER 8
'The People's Princess'

She was at peace. NOW, her face is peaceful, almost angelic. She looked stunning in her simple yet gorgeous outfit. She had many bangles around her wrists and a few of plain rings on her fingers. At the very end, the one man in her life who had never failed her down, the man she referred to as' my rock', her butler, Paul Burrell, remained by her side so that she would not be alone in the hours leading up to her final voyage. As Charles prayed and cried quiet tears by her casket in Kensington Palace, the entire world wept with him, still in disbelief and unable to absorb the stark and shocking news that Diana, Princess of Wales, had died. Only a few days ago, the public had loved viewing photos of her resting on her Mediterranean vacation with the new guy in her life, Dodi Fayed. She appeared comfortable with herself, and the audience was quietly pleased that a woman who had been through so much appeared to have found some personal happiness and joy. Many of her fans were quietly pleased by her zealous emphasis on humanitarian issues, particularly her anti-landmine campaign, and the notion that she had resolved many of the difficulties that had plagued her since her departure from the royal family. Earlier that summer, her choice to sell her royal clothing at a charity auction in New York was a very public hint that the Princess was ready to move on, that her new life, her real life, was just getting started. Indeed, encouraged by the auction's success, she had written to other pals, asking them to return the clothes she had given them. Some people received her request the morning after she died. The people sensed this sea change, making her sudden passing all the more difficult to take. The writer Adam Nicolson captured the mood: "The clutching dragging sadness felt by the world was the knowledge that this long hard struggle, so bravely and in some ways blindly fought, like a drowning person struggling for air, for the surface, for the light, should be cut off and shut down by the grim banality of a car crash." It's a disproportionate conclusion to everything that came before. That's why it aches. There was little comfort in knowing that the last few days of her life had been absolutely lovely, as she had spent her second holiday alone with Dodi Fayed, floating off the coast of Sardinia on his father's yacht Jonikal. They intended to end their trip with a night in Paris before Diana went back to Britain to see her boys. The trailing paparazzi had been a nuisance, openly clashing with the yacht's crew, but the couple's departure for Paris was expected. Nonetheless, when they landed at Le Bourget airport outside Paris on a steamy Saturday afternoon, cameras were waiting, as were vehicles and security personnel from Mohamed al-Fayed's Ritz hotel.

On their way to the five-star hotel, they stopped at the former Paris house of the Duke and Duchess of Windsor, another diamond in Fayed's crown, so Dodi could show the Princess around the meticulously renovated mansion and its magnificent grounds. During their voyage from the airport, they were followed by a group of photographers on motorcycles who buzzed her Mercedes in an attempt to capture photos of the couple. The bodyguard, Kes Wingfield, who was travelling in a backup security vehicle with Henri Paul and played a fateful role in their deaths, recalls that the Princess, while irritated by the attentions of photographers, was more concerned that one of the trailing cameramen would fall and injure himself due to the recklessness of their pursuit. That afternoon, she was thinking about more than just the paparazzi's behaviour. Once they arrived at the Ritz, the Princess received a phone call from an apprehensive Prince William, who had been requested to participate in a photo call at Eton, where he was about to begin his third year. While the Buckingham Palace request was part of an agreement between the press and the Palace that, in exchange for leaving the young princes alone, the media would be given occasional official photo opportunities, William was concerned that his younger brother, Prince Harry, would be overshadowed. Diana communicated her worries. As she had her hair done at the Ritz, she undoubtedly reflected on this, her final discussion with her eldest son. Meanwhile, at around 6.30 p.m., Dodi went to Alberto Repossi, a neighbouring jewellery store that had altered Diana's 'Tell Me Yes' ring while the pair was shopping in Monte Carlo during their Mediterranean cruise. Later that evening, they intended to visit Dodi's magnificent residence on the Champs-Élysées before dining at Le Benoît restaurant near the Pompidou Centre.

Was this where Dodi intended to declare his love, offer the ring that was later discovered in his room, and beg for Diana's hand in marriage? Certainly, their final chats with confidants that night indicated that their brief romance was going to take a serious and maybe permanent turn. Diana had already called Richard Kay, a Daily Mail correspondent who had grown to know her well since her first solo international trip to Nepal in 1993. As she spoke, he got the idea that she loved Dodi and he loved her. They were, he assumed, 'blissfully pleased'. That same evening, Dodi told the Saudi Arabian millionaire Hassan Yassin, Dodi's stepfather's brother, who was also staying at the Ritz, that "it's serious." We are planning to get married. Hassan subsequently stated, 'I was very thrilled for him, for both of them.'

Just after 7 p.m., the couple made the short drive to Dodi's flat, where they spent a few hours. Photographers saw them exiting the hotel and entering his apartment, where they later discovered her gifts of devotion, a cigar cutter and her father's cufflinks. The presence of prowling photographers prompted them to cancel their restaurant reservation and return to the Ritz for dinner. When they arrived at 9.50 p.m., Diana, dressed in a black blazer and white trousers, and Dodi, clad in a brown suede jacket, appeared uneasy, which was exacerbated by the looks of fellow diners as they sat down for dinner in the hotel's two-star Espadon restaurant. Instead, they returned to the Imperial Suite, which costs £6,000 per night, where Diana ate scrambled eggs with asparagus before moving on to soul. Meanwhile, Henri Paul, the hotel's deputy head of security, who had been off duty for three hours, was summoned to arrange for the couple's return to Dodi's apartment, where they were scheduled to spend the night. Dodi's love poetry was waiting for her in his flat, etched on a silver plaque. He'd carefully placed it under her pillow. She never saw it.

Meanwhile, the crowd of photographers waiting outside the hotel for the couple to emerge grew by the hour, and Henri Paul, who knew some of them by name, stepped outside on occasion to speak and tease them about when the pair might appear. His employer, Dodi Fayed, had different ideas. According to bodyguard Kes Wingfield, Dodi devised a strategy to conduct an operation that would leave the photographers empty-handed. The plan was easy enough: decoy cars would leave from the front of the Ritz, luring the paparazzi away, allowing Dodi and Diana to escape from the back and return unfettered to his flat. At 12.20 a.m., Diana, Dodi, driver Henri Paul, and another bodyguard, Trevor Rees-Jones, drove away from the hotel's rear service entrance. While Henri Paul allegedly told the handful of journalists, 'Don't bother following, you won't catch us,' photographers on foot were able to capture photos of the Princess, burying her face in her arms, as the car exited the hotel grounds.

Details of the next few minutes are unclear, with spokespeople from all sides twisting every piece of available data in an attempt to dodge responsibility for the terrible events of that night. The motorist, Henri Paul, was undeniably inebriated, three times the legal limit for drinking and driving. He had also taken a combination of medications, one an antidepressant and the other designed to treat alcoholism.

Based on the level of alcohol in his bloodstream, he was 600 times more likely to be involved in a deadly car accident than if he was sober. Henri Paul drove like a crazy, speeding through a densely populated area at reckless speeds, high on alcohol, drugs, and adrenaline, anxious to ensure that Dodi's decoy ploy worked. According to Dominic Lawson, the Sunday Telegraph editor and a friend of the Princess, 'Drunk or sober, no chauffeur would speed at over 100 miles per hour in a tunnel with a 30 mile per hour limit, unless directed to do so by his boss.'

At the Place de la Concorde, one trailing photographer saw Paul leap the Mercedes through a red light and accelerate towards the Place de l'Alma underpass on the north bank of the Seine. At roughly 12.24 a.m., the Mercedes entered the poorly illuminated tunnel at speeds ranging from 85 to 95 mph. Henri Paul lost control of the car, hitting head-on with an exposed concrete pillar separating the carriageways, sliding around and coming to a standstill facing the wrong way.

The driver and Dodi were killed instantaneously, but the bodyguard, the lone occupant wearing a seatbelt, was badly injured and regained consciousness after two weeks. The Princess was caught in the well between the front and back seats, fatally injured and unresponsive. The pursuing photographers arrived first, around 300 metres behind Diana, and reported hearing a bang so loud that they assumed she had been the victim of an assassin's bomb.

Frédéric Mailliez, a passing French doctor, offered emergency help but failed to recognize the scarcely breathing woman, who was, in his words, 'unconscious, wailing and waving in every direction'.

When more medical personnel arrived, several paparazzi lingered around the car, taking pictures. Romuald Rat, a skilled first-aider and photographer, entered the rear door, supposedly to check Diana's pulse, and soothed her in English. Others were less sympathetic, suggesting that the door was left open so that he and his colleagues could snap better images of the bloody scene. As the first partial testimonies emerged, many people were horrified to learn that the cameramen had neglected to comfort the dying Princess or call for medical help. Initial police reports depicted a chaotic scene with 'camera flashes going out like machine-gun fire around the back right hand side of the vehicle where the door was open.' The first police officers on the site had to ask for reinforcements to deal with the ferocious paparazzi, whose behaviour in pursuing Diana initially suggested that she had been hunted to death. Seven photographers were arrested and charged with manslaughter and failure to assist accident victims.

One of the many cruel ironies in Diana's tragic life was that, while still married to Prince Charles, one of her most cherished ambitions was to spend a weekend in Paris without bodyguards or photographers, losing herself in the crowd. Instead, as life slipped from her, with the Mercedes horn mournfully blaring into the night like a macabre 'Last Post', her adult life ended as it had begun, in the brazen, staccato embrace of the camera flash. Even in the city of dreams, she was unable to escape her past.

It took an hour for rescuers to stabilise her and pull her from the mangled wreckage before she was gently driven to the nearby La Pitié-Salpêtrière hospital for emergency surgery. By then, it was far too late. She had suffered severe head and chest injuries, and despite the best efforts of the medical team, they were unable to save her. She was pronounced dead at 4 a.m. (or 3 a.m. in London). A post-mortem investigation suggested that the Princess, who never regained consciousness, was probably dead some 20 minutes after the collision. Her mother, Frances Shand Kydd, stated days later: "I know the extent of her injuries, and I promise everyone that she knew nothing." She did not suffer at all.' She added: 'My knowledge comes first hand,' viewed as a retort to Mohamed al-Fayed who, the night before the funeral, publicised the fact that he had passed on Diana's purported last words and instructions to her elder sister, Lady Sarah McCorquodale, during a meeting at Harrods. Mrs Shand Kydd's dismissal of the 'last words' was backed up by a statement from the first doctor to arrive at the scene of the incident.

Shortly after the accident the Queen and Prince Charles, who were in Balmoral, were woken by staff and told that Diana had been gravely hurt. The Prince listened to radio updates all night but did not wake the lads until later in the morning when he delivered them the horrible news. 'I sensed something was wrong, I kept waking up all night,' Prince William was claimed to have stated. Similar news was sent to the Prime Minister, Tony Blair, and Diana's sisters, Lady Sarah McCorquodale and Lady Jane Fellowes, the wife of the Queen's private secretary, Sir Robert Fellowes. At 4.41am the world was informed of the horrible news in a quick newsflash. 'Diana, Princess of Wales has died, according to British sources, the Press Association learnt this morning.'

As the nation strained to fathom the enormity of their loss, the impulse to ascribe blame was the unavoidable handmaiden of their grief. Before it was determined that the driver was inebriated and speeding, it was the infamous paparazzi who were in the dock. Speaking from South Africa, Earl Spencer was the first to point a finger. Visibly upset by the waste of his sister's life he said: 'I always knew the press would kill her in the end. But not even I could imagine that they would take such a direct hand in her death as seems to be the case. It would appear that every proprietor and editor of every publication that has paid for intrusive and exploitative photographs of her, encouraging greedy and ruthless individuals to risk everything in pursuit of Diana's image, has blood on their hands today.'

He went on: 'Finally the one consolation is that Diana is now in a place where no human being can ever touch her again. I pray that she rests in peace.'

The Fayed family, too, were moved to action, lawyers acting for the family taking out a civil suit against the photographers who had been arrested at the scene. Their spokesman now denounced their activities. 'There is no doubt in Mr Fayed's mind that this tragedy would not have occurred but for the press photographers who have dogged Mr Fayed and the Princess for weeks.' The paparazzi, he said, behaved like 'Apache Indians swarming around a Wells Fargo stage-coach firing not arrows but flashlights into the driver's eyes.' Central to the discussion was whether the paparazzi had caused the crash as a direct result of their actions or obliquely, as a result of their unwelcome presence.

While the recriminations continued throughout a week that has proved to be a watershed in British history, in the first hours there were the practical matters of organising Diana's funeral and the sad task of bringing her body back from France. As a divorced Princess of Wales without a royal title, Palace courtiers were initially confused about her style and status, as unsure about how to treat her in death as in life. Certainly she could not be treated as any private citizen who had been killed abroad. The Queen and the Prince of Wales and their advisers were in full agreement, contrary to some reports, that she must be accorded full royal status.

Before he and Diana's sisters flew to Paris, the Prince joined the rest of the royal family, including Princes William and Harry, at Sunday service at Crathie church close to the Balmoral estate. The boys, who had been given the option of attending or not, insisted on taking part in the service. Although this lasted an hour, no mention was made of Diana's death nor were prayers spoken in remembrance. Instead, the minister stuck to his original sermon about the dubious joys of moving house, replete with jokes by the Scottish comedian, Billy Connolly. This was the first of many differences of tone and emphasis between the people and the Palace which at first jarred and then led to open resentment.

While the royal family were at prayer, Diana's butler, Paul Burrell, was one of a number of royal officials who flew to Paris to organise her homecoming. He carried a small suitcase containing her clothes and make-up, spending a long time preparing the body for the imminent arrival of the Prince of Wales and Diana's two sisters. When the royal party flew in, late in the afternoon, they were led to the first-floor casualty room where Diana's coffin lay. Each of the group spent a few minutes alone saying their private farewells, the Prince of Wales remaining with his former wife for 30 minutes. It was clear when they emerged that many tears had been shed.

On a day when millions of people around the world couldn't or wouldn't believe their princess had died, it wasn't until the BAe146 of the Queen's Flight made its final approach to RAF Northolt at 7 p.m. on Sunday, August 31, that the severity of her loss became clear. Her casket, covered in the Royal Standard and topped with a solitary bouquet of white flowers from her family, was carried silently across the tarmac by eight RAF pallbearers, watched by the Prime Minister and a number of other military and political dignitaries. While her remains were brought to a private mortuary and then to St James's Palace, her companion, Dodi Fayed, was buried at Brookwood Cemetery in Woking after a funeral at Regent's Park Mosque.

When the Prime Minister addressed the nation earlier in the day from his Sedgefield constituency, he nailed the sense of loss and grief, having been in direct communication with the Queen and Prince Charles. He spoke without notes, his voice shaking with emotion, describing Diana as a 'beautiful and kind human being'.

'She brought joy and comfort into the lives of countless people in Britain and around the world. We can only imagine how difficult things were for her at times. However, people all across the world, not just in Britain, continued to believe in Princess Diana. They liked her, adored her, and saw her as one of the people. She was the People's Princess, and she will remain so in all of our hearts and memories forever.

While his was the first of many tributes from world figures, it perfectly captured the mood of the nation during a historic week in which the British people, with sober intensity and angry dignity, put the ancien régime on trial, particularly an elitist, exploitative, and male-dominated media and an unresponsive monarchy. For a week, Britain bowed to flower power, with the aroma and sight of millions of bouquets serving as a silent and telling testament to the public's love for a lady reviled by the Establishment her whole life.

So it was totally fitting that Buckingham Palace declared her funeral will be 'a special service for a unique person'. The posies, poems, candles, and cards left at Kensington Palace, Buckingham Palace, and other locations said volumes about the nation's emotions and the situation of modern Britain. 'The royal family never valued you, but the people did,' read one note as thousands of individuals, the most of whom had never met her, paid modest homage at Kensington Palace to convey their loss, sorrow, remorse, and regret. Strangers hugged and comforted one another; some waited patiently to lay their tributes; and some prayed silently. When evening fell, the gardens were bathed in an ethereal radiance from thousands of candles, transforming them into a dignified pilgrimage site that Chaucer would have recognized. Everyone was welcome and came, a rainbow coalition of young and old of every colour and ethnicity, East Enders and West Enders, refugees, the disabled, the lonely, the curious, and, of course, droves of visitors. She was the only person in the kingdom who could connect with both the Britons who had been driven to the margins of society and those who ruled it.

Diana's life, her fragility, strength, frailty, beauty, compassion, and pursuit of fulfilment had affected, inspired, and ultimately moved them more than anything else in their lives. Not only did she capture the spirit of the time, mirroring society as the monarchy once did, but her life and death appeared to be part of a religious cycle of sin and redemption, a genuinely good and Christian woman martyred for our sins, exemplifying our strange appetite for celebrity. The artist Madonna admitted: "As much as I want to blame the press, we all have blood on our hands." All of us, including myself, bought and read these magazines. Even the quickly manufactured T-shirts with the mawkish sentiment: 'Born a princess, died a saint' accurately captured the popular mood less than a thousand days before the new century.

Those few days after her death forever captured the contrast between the Princess and the House of Windsor: her openness, their distance; her affection, their frigidity; her spontaneity, their inflexibility; hero glamour, their dullness; her modernity, their stale ritual; her emotional generosity, their aloofness; her rainbow coalition, their aristocratic court. Polly Toynbee, a commentator, stated that the Palace could handle Diana the Difficult, but not St Diana. If the monarchy eventually ends peacefully, Diana's ghostly presence will have played a role.

As the royal family spent the week in seclusion at Balmoral, they appeared to be a disturbed clan perplexed by circumstances, retiring from the nation rather than leading it in sorrow. While this was an entirely unjust assumption, the nation's rising dissatisfaction with their actions was not new. During the late 1980s, when Britain experienced a series of horrific disasters, most notably the Hillsborough football stadium tragedy, the Pan Am aeroplane crash at Lockerbie, and the sinking of the Marchioness pleasure cruiser, the royal family was conspicuously absent, preferring to stay on vacation rather than attend memorial services. They were heavily criticised at the time, but the fury subsided quickly. This time, the intensity of emotions threatened to overwhelm. It was maybe fortunate that a deer-stalking party scheduled for that week on the Balmoral estate did not take place.

While the church service at Crathie jarred, dissatisfaction grew as the Palace looked to be more concerned with procedure than with the wishes of the people. The people were irritated in a variety of tiny ways, including the police's initial refusal to allow bouquets to be placed outside Buckingham Palace, where the Union Flag, unlike those on practically every other public building in Britain, was not even flying at half mast. Those wishing to pay tribute had to wait up to 12 hours to sign one of St James' Palace's 5 books of condolences, which were later expanded to 43 amid public outrage. More crucial than the royal family's insufficient response to the public outpouring of grief was the sense that they were abandoning the nation at a critical time. The Queen's choice to arrive in London on Saturday morning for the funeral prompted historian Lord Blake to criticise courtiers for adhering too strictly to royal protocol. 'There will never be another Princess Diana,' he declared. The Sun tabloid was characteristically forthright, asking, "Where is the Queen when the country needs her?" She is 550 miles from London, the epicentre of the nation's mourning.

For once, this was not just a tabloid rant. In a way that spoke to the essence of a monarchy in a modern democratic state, the people wanted to see the Head of State unite and console, rather than observing from the wings. So there was a ripple of applause among the crowd outside Buckingham Palace when it was revealed that the Queen will come to the capital and address the country on the eve of the funeral. 'Our mother is returning home,' said one middle-aged guy, barely holding back tears. The compassion, warmth, and generosity of the Queen's homage, delivered from the first-floor balcony overlooking the Mall, silenced many carping tongues. She informed her television audience, "What I say to you now as your Queen and grandmother is from my heart." First, I'd like to pay respect to Diana herself. She was a remarkable and gifted human being. In good and difficult circumstances, she never lost the ability to grin and laugh, and her warmth and kindness inspired others. I admired and appreciated her for her energy and commitment to others, particularly her love for her two sons. She went on to say that at Balmoral that week, the royal family was attempting to help Princes William and Harry cope with the 'devastating loss' they had experienced.

The unprecedented decision to allow the Union Flag to fly at half mast over Buckingham Palace after the Queen had left to attend the funeral service, the agreement to double the length of the funeral route, and the walkabouts by the Queen and Prince Philip outside Buckingham Palace and by the Prince of Wales and his children outside Kensington Palace demonstrated that the Sovereign, her heir, and the Prime Minister were sensitive to what the Queen called the "extraordinar

While the Queen had risen triumphantly from the shadows, it was Prince William, the torchbearer of Diana's legacy, who was the true object of adoration. When he joined his father and brother at the gates of Kensington Palace, this shyly smiling, dignified young man was received with the kind of genuflecting rapture more appropriate for a Papal visit, with some women crying as they kissed his hand.

Diana's leaving showed her fervent mood. Her funeral was, in sight and sound, more mediaeval than modern; there was the doleful sound of the tenor bell that tolled every minute as Diana's coffin, borne on a horse-drawn gun carriage, made its sombre way from Kensington Palace to Westminster Abbey; the straining silence of the crowd; the ancient solemnity of the Christian service; and the strewing of flowers along the road as Diana's body was taken to Althorp where, after a private ceremony, she was laid to rest.

Even Earl Spencer's rapier thrusts at the royal family during his funeral oration elicited groans of applause from the throng outside, reminiscent of an impudent Earl of Essex daring to challenge Elizabeth I in front of her Court. The picture of Princes William and Harry following the rumbling gun carriage captured the immediacy of their bereavement, presenting the Spencers and Windsors as two families grieving together rather than distant, shimmering characters.

While the style was archaic, almost tribal, historians will remember September 6, 1997, as the day when the old hierarchical regime crumbled and a new egalitarian period began. When the Queen bowed to Diana's coffin as it passed Buckingham Palace, she was paying homage not only to Diana but also to everything she represented, principles that embody so much of modern Britain - 'The stiff upper lip vs the trembling lower lip,' as one wag put it.

If Elton John's impassioned song of 'Candle in the Wind', modified to include a tribute to Diana, captured everyone's sentiments, Earl Spencer communicated the nation's opinions with a cutting and remorseless honesty. He threw down the challenge to the Sovereign and her family, as well as the assembled Fourth Estate, tacitly chastising the royal family for seizing Diana's title and raising their children. Diana, he claimed, 'needs no royal title to continue to conjure her special brand of enchantment,' referring to the fact that the Queen had stripped the Princess of her right to be styled as 'Her Royal Highness' after she divorced. It came as little surprise that when his brother-in-law, the Queen's private secretary, Sir Robert Fellowes, delivered the offer to reestablish her honorary title later that day, her brother flatly refused.

Earl Spencer did not spare the Windsors from their track record when it came to raising children. 'On behalf of your mother and sisters, I pledge that we, your blood family, will do everything we can to continue the imaginative and loving way in which you were steering these two exceptional young men, so that their souls are not simply immersed in duty and tradition, but can sing openly as you intended.'

After effortlessly mocking the Windsors as a dysfunctional family, he went on to hammer the mass media. 'My only explanation [for her media treatment] is that true goodness threatens people on the opposite extreme of the moral spectrum. It is worth remembering that, of all the ironies concerning Diana, maybe the biggest was this: a girl named after the ancient goddess of hunting ended up being the most hunted person of the contemporary era.

While these sentiments elicited spontaneous applause from the congregation, he spoke with insight about his sister, whom he described as 'the unique, the complex, the extraordinary, and irreplaceable Diana whose beauty, both internal and external, will never be extinguished from our minds.' He commended her compassion, flair, intuition, and sensitivity, but admitted that her eating disorders were caused by underlying sentiments of insecurity and unworthiness.

Her brother, like the royal family, her friends, and counsellors, was taken aback by the outpouring of sadness following her death, and he warned against canonising her memory. 'You stand tall enough as a human being with unique attributes not to be regarded as a saint,' he stated.

It was a futile hope. Diana entered the pantheon of the immortals as a memorial fund in her memory raised hundreds of millions of pounds, as Elton John's Diana tribute became the fastest- and biggest-selling single of all time, and as books, DVDs, magazines, and other paraphernalia surfaced. Like Elvis Presley's Graceland, her final resting place in Althorp has become a site of pilgrimage and respect. She has received numerous posthumous awards, including the Nobel Peace Prize, and her name has been lent to hospitals, hospices, and other charitable causes all over the world, while her work and memory continue to inspire many members of this generation to live more meaningful and fulfilled lives.

It is evident that there are two Dianas: the person known to her friends and family, and the revered icon, the projection of millions of fantasies, hopes and desires. Many of those who knew her as a little girl, a troubled princess, and a divorcee looking for happiness are still perplexed by the worldwide outpouring of sadness. Her death did not elicit the type of mass hysteria that is common at pop events, but rather something far more profound. Many doctors are referring to 'the Diana Syndrome' as they work with distressed members of the public who have come to them for therapy after the Princess' death triggered traumatic emotions buried deep within them.

So, how do we describe Diana as both an individual and a phenomenon? Diana was a complex web of contradictions throughout her life: fearless yet frail, unloved but adored, needy but generous, self-obsessed yet selfless, inspirational yet despairing, demanding advice but disliking criticism, honest yet disingenuous, intuitive yet unworldly, supremely sophisticated yet constantly uncertain, and manipulative but naive. She could be stubborn, aggravating, a flawed perfectionist who would disarm with a self-deprecating witticism; her penetrating, cornflower-blue eyes enticed with a glance. Her language had no limitations; her lexicon consisted of the grin, caress, hug, and kiss, rather than the statement or speech. She was endlessly fascinating and will be forever enigmatic.

Throughout her life, she was directed by instinct and intuition rather than argument or discussion. A river led her on a voyage into the worlds of astrologers, psychics, soothsayers, and therapists. Here is the key to unlocking the doors between her personality and her worldwide appeal. This is why, if Diana had lived indefinitely, the media would have never understood or appreciated her. Because she was not from their world and did not share their ideals. When she gazed at a rose, she admired its beauty, and they counted the petals.

Diana's work welcomed those on the outskirts of society, such as lepers, Aids victims, and others, and much of her appeal stemmed from the way she tapped into a spiritual undercurrent in society, a fundamentally feminine attitude to living that had been driven underground for ages. Hers was an appeal to our emotional rather than cerebral intelligence, her intuitive and caring nature, and the way she had been used and exploited by men throughout her life, whether princes or photographers, reflecting how many women saw their own lives. At her core, she was a feminist who championed feminine principles rather than seeking acceptability in a male-dominated society. Her significance now lies not just in what she accomplished during her lifetime, but also in the meaning of her existence and the inspiration she provided to others, particularly women, in their search for their own truth.

As historians consider her notoriety and legacy, they will come to see Diana, Princess of Wales as one of the most influential figures of this, or any other, era. For as long as there are poets, playwrights, and men with broken hearts, stories will be told about the princess who died across the river and returned home to be crowned queen, the queen of all our hearts.

Diana, the Princess of Wales. She wrote poetry in our souls. And made us wonder.

The contents of this book may not be copied, reproduced or transmitted without the express written permission of the author or publisher. Under no circumstances will the publisher or author be responsible or liable for any damages, compensation or monetary loss arising from the information contained in this book, whether directly or indirectly. .

Disclaimer Notice:

Although the author and publisher have made every effort to ensure the accuracy and completeness of the content, they do not, however, make any representations or warranties as to the accuracy, completeness, or reliability of the content. , suitability or availability of the information, products, services or related graphics contained in the book for any purpose. Readers are solely responsible for their use of the information contained in this book

Every effort has been made to make this book possible. If any omission or error has occurred unintentionally, the author and publisher will be happy to acknowledge it in upcoming versions.

Made in United States
Cleveland, OH
16 April 2025

16131791R00085